READY TO WRITE

A First
Composition
Text

THIRD EDITION

Karen Blanchard

Christine Root

Longman

This book is dedicated to the memory of Karen's father, Dr. Herbert Lourie, whose love of learning was an inspiration to all who knew him; and to the memory of Christine's mother, Charlotte S. Baker, who understood so well the power and magic of the written word.

Pearson Education, 10 Bank Street, White Plains, NY 10606

Vice President, director of instructional design: Allen Ascher
Senior acquisitions editor: Laura Le Dréan
Development director: Penny Laporte
Development editor: Paula H. Van Ells
Vice president, director of design and production: Rhea Banker
Director of electronic production: Aliza Greenblatt
Executive managing editor: Linda Moser
Production manager: Ray Keating
Production editor: Michael Mone
Director of manufacturing: Patrice Fraccio
Senior manufacturing buyer: Dave Dickey
Photo research: Mykan White
Cover design: Pat Wosczyk
Text design: Patrice Sheridan, Pat Wosczyk
Text composition: Paula D. Williams
Illustrations: Susan Detrich
Text art: pp. 5, 42, 49, 55, 56, 57, 64, 65, 76, 87, 88, 89, 90, 91, 92, 105, 107, 108, 110, 118, 119, 129, 130, 131, 132, 134, 137, 138, 139, 141, 143, Paula Williams; Lisa Ghiozzi, pp. 24, 34, 36, 37, 38, 50, 52, 53, 66, 100, 106, Kenneth Batelman
Text and photo credits: Page 20. Reproduced from the Ladybird book Talk about Holidays with the permission of the publishers, Ladybird Books Limited. Loughborough,England. Page 52. Reprinted with permission from Open Doors: 2001, The Institute of International Education. Page 53. Adapted from The Complete Book of Running, by James F. Fixx, © 1977 by Random House, Inc. Page 59. Adapted from The Bow Tie Book by Mario Sartori © 1986 by Simon & Schuster, Inc. Page 72. Photo by Linda Borish. Reprinted with permission. Page 77. Photo by Seth G. Schofield. Reprinted with permission. Page 110. Photo courtesy of David Root. Page 127. From the Golden Stamp Book of Earth and Ecology by George S. Fichter © 1972 Western Publishing Company, Inc. Page 137. Photo courtesy of David Root. Page 139. Adapted by permission of News for You, published by New Readers Press, publishing division of Laubach Literacy International, 1320 Jamesville Ave., Syracuse, New York 13210, July 7, 1982. PEANUTS reprinted by permission of United Feature Syndicate, Inc.

Library of Congress Cataloging-in-Publication Data

Blanchard, Karen Lourie, 1951-
    Ready to write: a first composition text / Karen Blanchard, Christine Root. --3rd ed
      p. cm.
    ISBN 0-13-042463-3 (alk. paper)
  1. English language--Textbooks for foreign speakers. 2. English
language--Composition and exercises. 3. Report writing--Problems, exercises, etc.
I. Root, Christine Baker, 1945- II. Title.

PE1128 .B587 2002
808'.042--dc21
                                                 2002075475

ISBN: 0-13-042463-3

Printed in the United States of America
3 4 5 6 7 8 9 10—BAH—07 06 05 04 03

Contents

Introduction

Ready to Write came about because of our threefold conviction that:

- high-beginning and low-intermediate students learn to write well and achieve a more complete English proficiency by learning and practicing writing skills simultaneously with other English language skills they are learning;

- students are interested in and capable of writing expressively in English, however simple the language, on a variety of provocative and sophisticated topics if they are supplied with the basic vocabulary and organizational tools;

- ESL students need to be explicitly taught that different languages organize information differently, and they need to be shown how to organize information correctly in English.

APPROACH

Based on these assumptions, *Ready to Write* is intended to get students writing early in their second language acquisition experience. By providing them with a wide variety of stimulating writing topics and exercises that go beyond sentence manipulation drills, students are encouraged to bring their own ideas and talent to the writing process. With a focus on the process of writing paragraphs, students learn, step by step, the organizational principles that will help them express themselves effectively in English. They also learn to apply these principles to a variety of rhetorical formats.

As in *Get Ready to Write* and *Ready to Write More*, the activities are designed to encourage students to think independently as well as provide them with many opportunities to share ideas with their classmates, thus creating a more dynamic learning environment. To this end, collaborative writing and peer feedback activities are included in all the chapters. In addition, great care has been taken to maintain an appropriate level of vocabulary and complexity of sentence structure for high-beginning and low-intermediate students so that the explanations, directions, and readings are easily accessible.

THE THIRD EDITION

This third edition of *Ready to Write* features:

- attention to different patterns of organization through the use of **model paragraphs**

- guidance and practice in recognizing and writing the **parts of the paragraph**

- guided practice in each stage of the paragraph writing process, including specific techniques for **prewriting**, **writing**, and **revising**

- numerous and varied **paragraph-writing** opportunities

- attention to **style** through presentations and activities on coherence, transitions, and the use of signal words

Two popular features from the previous editions "You Be the Editor" and "On Your Own" continue to appear regularly in this edition. "You Be the Editor" provides practice in error correction and proofreading in order to help students monitor their own errors. (An Answer Key for this section is at the end of this book.) "On Your Own" provides students with further individual practice in the paragraph-writing skills they have learned. We hope that you enjoy working through these activities with your students. At any level, they are definitely ready to write. KLB and CBR

CHAPTER 1

Organization: The Key to Good Writing

Writing can be difficult even in your own language. In a new language, writing can be even more difficult. The good news is that writing involves skills that you can learn, practice, and master. As you work through this book, you will learn and practice skills you need to become a good writer in English.

Organization is the key to good writing. Different languages organize ideas differently. In this chapter, you will begin to learn how to organize information in English so that you can write effective paragraphs.

Organizing by Grouping

Look at the following list of places.

South America   Asia
New York City   Tokyo
Italy   Mexico
Korea   Europe
Istanbul

This list can be organized by dividing it into three groups.

A	B	C
South America	Italy	New York City
Asia	Korea	Istanbul
Europe	Mexico	Tokyo

1. What do all the places in group A have in common?
   <u>They are continents.</u>

2. What do all the places in group B have in common?
   _____

3. What do all the places in group C have in common?
   _____

Each group can be further organized by giving it a name.

A	B	C
CONTINENTS	**COUNTRIES**	**CITIES**
South America	Italy	New York City
Asia	Korea	Istanbul
Europe	Mexico	Tokyo

ORGANIZING LISTS

A. Organize each list of words by dividing it into three groups. Put similar ideas together and give each group a name. One list has been done for you.

1. ~~Sunday~~
   January
   February
   summer
   ~~Tuesday~~
   winter
   spring
   ~~Friday~~
   December

A	B	C
Name: ___days___	Name: _____	Name: _____
Sunday	_____	_____
Tuesday	_____	_____
Friday	_____	_____

2. jet
   bus
   boat
   car
   airplane
   truck
   helicopter
   submarine
   ship

A	B	C
Name: _____	Name: _____	Name: _____
_____	_____	_____
_____	_____	_____
_____	_____	_____

3. Spanish
   calculus
   biology
   algebra
   Japanese
   chemistry
   Arabic
   geometry
   physics

A	B	C
Name: _____	Name: _____	Name: _____
_____	_____	_____
_____	_____	_____
_____	_____	_____

4. ring   glasses
    hat   mittens
    shoes   boots
    socks   headband
    gloves

A	B	C
Name: _____	Name: _____	Name: _____
_____	_____	_____
_____	_____	_____
_____	_____	_____

B. Often there is more than one way to organize things. Study the following list.

wine   pork   whiskey
roast beef   carrots   spinach
milk   beer   juice
potatoes   chicken   coffee

1. First divide the list into *two* groups and give each group a name.

A	B
Name: _____	Name: _____
_____	_____
_____	_____
_____	_____
_____	_____

2. Now divide each group again. Give each new group a name.

A	B
Name: _____	Name: _____
_____	_____
_____	_____
_____	_____

C	D
Name: _____	Name: _____
_____	_____
_____	_____
_____	_____

Can you think of something else to add to each group?

Topics

When you organized the lists, you put similar items together. You also gave each group a name. The name is the topic.

CHOOSING A TOPIC

One word in each list is more general than the others. This word is the topic of the list. Circle the topic.

Example

Spanish
Japanese
Arabic
(Language)
English

A	B	C
Volkswagen	tennis	Lincoln
Cars	soccer	Presidents
Volvo	sports	Clinton
Mercedes	baseball	Kennedy
Ford	football	Bush

D	E
occupations	flowers
dentist	trees
teacher	vegetation
lawyer	plants
engineer	grass

WRITING A TOPIC

Write a topic for each list.

A	B	C
_____	_____	_____
Atlantic	four	apple
Pacific	seventeen	orange
Indian	fifty	banana
	three hundred	peach

Irrelevant Information

When you organize your information into groups, it is important to recognize when something does not belong. When something does not belong, it is called *irrelevant*.

IDENTIFYING IRRELEVANT INFORMATION

A. Cross out the item in each group that does not belong.

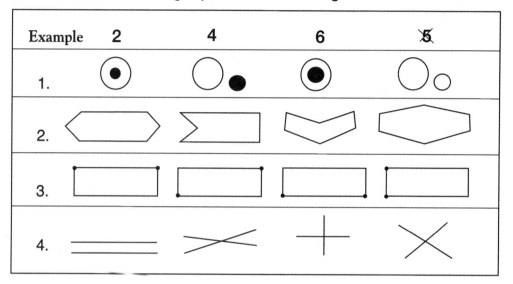

B. Cross out the word in each of the following groups that does not belong. Then write a topic for each list.

Example   *food*
            candy
            chicken
            ~~flowers~~
            vegetables

1. _____   2. _____   3. _____   4. _____

   green   Pennsylvania   desk   Spanish

   dress   Philadelphia   chair   Turkish

   yellow   Florida   table   Chinese

   blue   California   book   Modern

5. _____   6. _____   7. _____   8. _____

   physics   February   computer   tire

   swimming   Wednesday   telephone   horn

   biology   April   fax machine   steering wheel

   chemistry   June   washing machine   Volkswagen

c. Cross out the sentence in each group that does not belong.

Example   **Topic:** It is interesting to visit foreign countries.

    a. You can meet new people.

    b. You can eat different kinds of food.

    c. ~~It is expensive.~~

    d. You can see the way other people live.

1. **Topic:** There is a lot to do in New York City.

    a. There are many museums to see.

    b. It is the cultural center of the United States.

    c. The subways are dirty.

    d. There are many kinds of restaurants.

2. **Topic:** People prefer small cars for a number of reasons.

    a. They are cheaper to buy.

    b. They use less gas than bigger cars.

    c. They are easier to park.

    d. Some small cars do not have enough legroom.

3. **Topic:** Different people spend their free time in different ways.

    a. A lot of people spend their free time going to movies.

    b. The price of movies has increased recently.

    c. Some people like to read.

    d. Many people enjoy sports.

    e. Some people prefer to listen to music.

4. **Topic:** Smoking cigarettes is a bad habit.

    a. It is expensive.

    b. It may cause cancer.

    c. There are many kinds of cigarettes.

    d. The smoke often bothers other people.

    e. Burning cigarettes cause fires.

CLASS ACTIVITY

Make a list of all the people in your class. Organize the list by dividing the people into groups. There are many ways to do this. For example, you can have one group for females and another for males. How many ways can you think of to organize your classmates? Remember that all members of a group should have something in common.

On Your Own

1. Make a list of things you have to do this weekend. Organize the items on your list into groups. Give each group a name.

2. Make a list of all the things you *should* do when you are learning a new language. Make another list of all the things you *shouldn't* do.

CHAPTER 2

Understanding Paragraphs

Most English writing is organized into paragraphs. A paragraph is a group of sentences that develops one main idea. It usually begins with a sentence that states the main idea. This sentence is called the topic sentence. The other sentences in the paragraph explain the main idea. They add details and give support. These sentences are called supporting sentences. Sometimes paragraphs also have a concluding sentence. It is the last sentence of the paragraph.

Read the model paragraph and study the parts.

    The students in the class come from many different parts of the world. Some are from European countries such as France, Spain, and Italy. Others are from Middle Eastern countries like Saudi Arabia and Israel. Still other students were born in Asian countries, including Japan and Korea. The largest number of students are from Latin American countries like Mexico, Venezuela, and Peru. The class is an interesting mix of people from many different countries.

topic sentence

supporting sentences

concluding sentence

A paragraph also needs to be in proper paragraph form. Follow these rules of proper paragraph form.

- Indent the first word of each paragraph.
- Leave margins (space on both sides of the paragraph).
- Begin each sentence with a capital letter.
- End each sentence with a period, question mark, or exclamation point.
- Do not start each new sentence on a new line.

Identifying Parts of a Paragraph

Read the following paragraphs and answer the questions.

1.   There are many reasons why people move. Some move to find better jobs or to advance their careers. Others are attracted to places with better weather. Still others want to move to a place with less crime. Finally, people often want to move to a place with a lower cost of living. For these reasons, every year millions of people pack up and move to new places.

   a. What is the topic sentence?

   _____

   b. How many supporting sentences are there in the paragraph? _____

   c. Is there a concluding sentence? _____

2.   Many men are now employed in jobs that traditionally belonged to women. For example, there are now twice as many male nurses as there were ten years ago. The number of male flight attendants has increased from zero in 1960 to over 10,000 today. Similarly, there are many more male secretaries, elementary school teachers, and telephone operators than ever before. It is clear that ideas about traditionally female occupations have changed.

   a. What is the topic sentence?

   _____

   b. How many supporting sentences are there in the paragraph? _____

   c. Is there a concluding sentence? _____

3.   For thousands of years garlic has had many uses. The Romans gave garlic to their slaves for strength and to their soldiers for courage. During the Middle Ages, some people used garlic to keep witches away. In the eighteenth century, garlic was used to cure diseases. Even today, some people believe that eating garlic can prevent colds. Garlic has a long history as a plant that can give health and protection.

   a. What is the topic sentence?

   _____

   b. How many supporting sentences are there in the paragraph? _____

   c. Is there a concluding sentence? _____

Topic Sentences

The topic sentence is the most important sentence of a paragraph. It states the main idea and introduces the reader to the topic.

CHOOSING A TOPIC SENTENCE

Choose the best topic sentence for each group of supporting sentences. Write it on the line provided.

Example

    _Skiing is my favorite sport_____. I usually go skiing every weekend in the winter even though it is expensive. I love the feeling of flying down a mountain. The views are beautiful from the top of a mountain and along the trails. Even the danger of falling and getting hurt can't keep me away from the slopes on a winter day.

  a. Skiing is expensive.
  b. Skiing is my favorite sport.
  c. Skiing is dangerous.

1. _____

North Americans send cards for many occasions. They send cards to family and friends on birthdays and holidays. They also send thank-you cards, get well cards, graduation cards, and congratulation cards. It is very common to buy cards in stores and send them through the mail, but turning on the computer and sending cards over the Internet is also popular.

  a. Sending cards is very popular in North America.
  b. Birthday cards are the most popular kind of card.
  c. It is important to send thank-you cards.

2. _____

I enjoy summer sports like water skiing and baseball, The weather is usually sunny and hot, so I can go to the beach almost every day. Gardening is my hobby and I spend many summer days working in my garden. Unfortunately, the days pass too quickly in summer.

  a. I like to garden in the summer.
  b. Summer is my favorite season.
  c. Summer is too short.

3. _____

First of all, we need money to repair old roads and build new roads. We also need more money to pay teachers' salaries and to pay for services such as trash collection. Finally, more tax money is needed to give financial help to the poor citizens of the city. It is clear that the city will have serious problems if taxes are not raised soon.

  a. We should raise city taxes.
  b. City taxes are too high.
  c. City taxes pay for new roads.

4. _____

For example, a person can have breakfast in New York, board an airplane, and have dinner in Paris. A businesswoman in London can instantly place an order with a factory in Hong Kong by sending a fax. Furthermore, a schoolboy in Tokyo can turn on a TV and watch a baseball game being played in Los Angeles.

   a. Airplanes have changed our lives.
   b. Advances in technology have made the world seem smaller.
   c. The fax machine was an important invention.

5. _____

One thing you must consider is the quality of the university's educational program. You also need to think about the school's size and location. Finally, you must be sure to consider the university's tuition to make sure you can afford to go to school there.

   a. It is expensive to attend a university in the United States.
   b. There are several factors to consider when you choose a university to attend.
   c. You should consider getting a good education.

WRITING A TOPIC SENTENCE

Write a topic sentence for each paragraph. Make sure your topic sentence expresses the main idea of the paragraph. Then share your topic sentences with your classmates by writing them on the chalkboard. Discuss the differences.

Example

Miami is the perfect place to take a vacation . It is always sunny and warm. The beaches are gorgeous, with soft white sand and beautiful water. There are many fine restaurants in the Miami area, and most of the hotels offer terrific entertainment nightly. It's no wonder that Miami is my first choice for a vacation destination.

1. _____.

He has collected stamps and coins ever since he was a child. He is very proud of his valuable collections. Paul also enjoys painting and drawing. Recently he has become interested in gardening. Out of all his hobbies, Paul's favorite one is reading. He usually reads at least one book every week. Paul keeps busy with all of his hobbies.

2. _____.

I can't wait to come home from school and eat the delicious meals she has prepared. She is famous for her desserts like peach pie and chocolate soufflé. She is always experimenting with new recipes and trying different ingredients. No one in the world can cook the way my mother does.

3. _____.

It never starts in cold weather. The horn and the left turn signal don't work properly. Worst of all, the radio only gets one station and the CD player is completely broken. I wish I could get a new car.

4. _____.

First, and most importantly, the work is very interesting. I learn new things every day and I get to travel a lot. In addition, my boss is very nice. She is always willing to help me when I have a problem. I have also made many new friends at my job. Last, but not least, the salary is fantastic.

5. _____.

To start things off, my plane was six hours late. When I finally got to my hotel, I was very disappointed. It was small and dirty. On the third day, my wallet was stolen, and I lost all my credit cards. It rained every day except one, and on that day I got a terrible sunburn. All in all, it wasn't a vacation to remember.

Supporting Sentences

The supporting sentences develop the main idea in the topic sentence. They add details to the topic.

RECOGNIZING SUPPORTING SENTENCES

Read the following paragraphs and underline the supporting sentences.

1.   Use of the Internet has grown very quickly. In 1983, there were 562 computers connected to the Internet. By the turn of the century, there were 72.3 million computers in 247 countries on-line. Experts say that the Internet is now growing at a rate of approximately 40 percent a year. As time goes on, the Internet is becoming more and more popular.

2.   There are many reasons I hate my apartment. The plumbing doesn't work properly and the landlord refuses to fix it. I also have noisy neighbors who keep me up all night. Furthermore, there are so many bugs in my apartment that I could start an insect collection. I really want to move!

3.   Vegetables and fruits are an important part of a healthy diet. First, fruits and vegetables are packed with the vitamins and minerals you need to keep your body functioning smoothly. In addition, they give you the carbohydrates you need for energy. Fruits and vegetables have lots of fiber to help your digestive system work properly. Finally, many scientists believe that the nutrients in fruits and vegetables can help fight diseases. If you eat a diet rich in fruits and vegetables, you'll be on the road to better health.

IDENTIFYING TOPIC AND SUPPORTING SENTENCES

Springfield Academy

A. **Read the following sentences about Springfield Academy, a boarding school for high school students. Some of the sentences are about the quality of education. Label these Q. Some are about the rules of the school. Label these R. With some of your classmates, read and discuss all of the sentences.**

1. ____   Springfield Academy is famous for the high quality of its education.

2. ____ Students are not allowed to leave campus without permission.

3. ____ Students are required to wear uniforms.

4. ____ The laboratories have the newest computers and equipment.

5. ____ Stereos and televisions cannot be played after 7 P.M.

6. ____ Most of its graduates attend very good universities.

7. ____ Many of the students at Springfield Academy feel that the rules are too strict and old-fashioned.

8. ____ Students who do not maintain a B average are put on probation.

9. ____ The library is one of the finest in the state.

B. Now divide the sentences into two groups. Remember to put similar ideas together.

Quality of Education

_____

_____

_____

_____

_____

_____

_____

Rules of the School

_____

_____

_____

_____

_____

_____

_____

One sentence in each group is general enough to be a topic sentence. Find that sentence in each group and circle it.

C. Use the sentences in each group to write two paragraphs. Put the topic sentences first. Review the rules of proper paragraph form on page 8.

Quality of Education

_____

_____

_____

_____

_____

Rules of the School

_____

_____

_____

_____

_____

San Francisco

A. Read the following sentences about San Francisco. Two of the sentences are topic sentences, and the rest are supporting sentences. Write *TS* in front of each topic sentence and *SS* in front of each supporting sentence.

1. _____ San Francisco is usually warm and pleasant during the day.

2. _____ Some of the country's most famous restaurants and hotels are in San Francisco.

3. _____ There are many things to see and do in San Francisco.

4. _____ The city has many interesting tourist attractions.

5. _____ There are many excellent art galleries.

6. _____ The weather in San Francisco is very pleasant.

7. _____ It is never too hot or too cold.

8. _____ The nightlife is exciting.

9. _____ San Francisco has a ballet company, an opera house, and a symphony orchestra.

10. _____ It is cool and breezy at night.

11. _____ The winters are mild and it rarely snows.

B. Write the two topic sentences on the lines provided. Then list the relevant supporting sentences under the topic sentences.

Topic Sentence	**Topic Sentence**
_____	_____
_____	_____
Supporting Sentences	**Supporting Sentences**
_____	_____
_____	_____
_____	_____
_____	_____
_____	_____
_____	_____
_____	_____
_____	_____

C. Write the sentences from the first group in paragraph form. Remember to indent the first sentence.

_____

_____

_____

_____

_____

_____

D. Now write the sentences from the second group in paragraph form.

_____

_____

_____

_____

_____

_____

Irrelevant Sentences

Every supporting sentence in a paragraph must relate to the main idea stated in the topic sentence. A sentence that does not support the main idea does not belong in the paragraph. When a sentence does not belong in a paragraph, it is called an _irrelevant sentence_.

Now read this paragraph again. Which sentence does not belong? Cross out the irrelevant sentence.

  The students in the class come from many different parts of the world. Some are from European countries, such as France, Spain, and Italy. Others are from Middle Eastern countries like Saudi Arabia and Israel. Still other students were born in Asian countries, including Japan and Korea. Korean food is delicious. The largest number of students are from Latin American countries like Mexico, Venezuela and Peru. The class is an interesting mix of people from many different countries.

The main idea of the paragraph is that the students in the class come from many different parts of the world. The fact that Korean food is delicious is true, but it does not support the main idea.

There is one irrelevant sentence in each paragraph that follows. Find that sentence and cross it out.

1.   Cats make wonderful house pets. They are very loving and friendly. Cats are also clean. They don't eat much, so they are not expensive. Unfortunately, some people are allergic to their hair. Cats look beautiful and they're fun to have in your home.

2.   There are several ways people can conserve natural resources. One way is to turn off lights and appliances when they are not in use. Another way is to drive cars less. My favorite kind of car is a convertible. People can also insulate their houses better. Finally, by reusing things like bottles and plastic bags, people can reduce the amount of waste. By practicing these simple guidelines, we can save our natural resources.

3.   The capital city of a country is usually a very important city. The government offices are located in the capital city and political leaders usually live there or nearby. There are many different types of governments in the world. The capital may also be the center of culture. There are often museums, libraries, and universities in the capital. Finally, the capital city can serve as a center of trade, industry, and commerce, so it is often the financial center of the country.

4.   The Japanese automobile industry uses robots in many stages of its production process. In fact, one large Japanese auto factory uses robots in all of its production stages. Some Japanese universities are developing medical robots to detect certain kinds of cancer. Another automobile factory in Japan uses them to paint cars as they come off the assembly line. Furthermore, most Japanese factories use robots to weld the parts of the finished car together.

5.   The packaging of many products is very wasteful. Often the packaging is twice as big as the product. Packaging is used to protect things that are breakable. Many food items, for example, have several layers of extra packaging. Most of these extra layers could be eliminated.

Concluding Sentences

Some paragraphs end with a concluding sentence. This sentence states the main idea of the paragraph again using different words. It summarizes the main points of the paragraph, or makes a final comment on the topic. Concluding sentences are not always necessary. In fact, short paragraphs or paragraphs that are part of longer pieces of writing often do not have concluding sentences.

WRITING CONCLUDING SENTENCES

Write a concluding sentence for each paragraph.

1.   There are many reasons why I like wearing a uniform to school. First of all, it saves time. I don't have to spend time picking out my clothes every morning. Wearing a uniform also saves money. It's cheaper to purchase a few uniforms than to go out and buy lots of school clothes. In addition, I don't have the

pressure of keeping up with the latest styles. Most importantly, wearing a school uniform gives me a sense that I belong. I really think it adds to the feeling of school spirit and community.

_____

_____

2.   There are many reasons why I am against wearing my school uniform. For one thing, I don't like the style of the uniform. The navy blazer and plaid skirt are too conservative for me. Secondly, the uniform isn't comfortable. I prefer to wear baggy pants and a sweater instead of a skirt and jacket. Finally, I want the freedom to express my individuality through my style of dressing.

_____

_____

3.   Credit cards have a lot of advantages. First of all, credit cards are convenient because you don't have to carry a lot of cash around. You can buy the products and services you need even if you do not have cash in your pocket. In addition, credit cards are very helpful in emergencies. Finally, you can become a better money manager as you learn to use credit cards responsibly.

_____

_____

CLASS ACTIVITY

A. Your teacher will write this topic sentence on the board.

It is difficult to learn a new language.

B. What details can you and your classmates think of to support this topic sentence? As you think of ideas, your teacher will write them in list form on the board. (Remember, these are just ideas, so they don't have to be complete sentences or in correct order.) Copy the list here.

_____   _____

_____   _____

_____   _____

C. Discuss the list with your classmates. Cross out details that don't belong.

D. With your classmates and teacher, choose the relevant ideas from the list above. Write them in sentence form on the board. Copy the sentences below.

_____

_____

_____

_____

_____

E. With your classmates and teacher, organize the sentences and put them in correct paragraph form. Your teacher will write the paragraph on the board. Copy the finished paragraph below.

_____

_____

_____

_____

_____

INDIVIDUAL ACTIVITY

A. Choose one of the following topic sentences to write about. Make a list of supporting details. You do not have to write the list in complete sentences.

- Exercise is necessary for good health.
- Eating in restaurants is expensive.
- It is important for parents to teach their children about _____.
- _____ is a great place to visit.

Topic sentence: _____

Supporting Details:

_____   _____

_____   _____

_____   _____

B. Cross out any irrelevant details.

C. Write the items on your list in complete sentences.

_____

_____

_____

_____

D. Write a paragraph based on your list.

READY TO WRITE

_____

_____

_____

_____

_____

_____

On Your Own

Write a paragraph about one of the following topics.

- my proudest moment
- my job
- my worst day
- my favorite kind of music
- babies
- my _____

1. Write a topic sentence.

2. Make a list of supporting details.

3. Think about the ideas on your list. Cross out any idea that does not support your topic sentence.

4. Write your list in complete sentences.

5. Use the topic and supporting sentences to write a paragraph.

CHAPTER 3

Organizing Information by Time

In Chapter 1, you learned that organization is the key to good writing. There are several ways to organize sentences in a paragraph. Three of the most common ways are time order, order of importance, and space order. In this chapter you will practice organizing ideas by time.

Time Order

When you tell a story, you organize the events in the story by time. You tell what happened first at the beginning of the story. Then you tell what happened second, third, and so on. In writing, you often do the same thing.

Look at the pictures. They tell a story, but they are not in the right time order. Number the pictures so they tell the story in a logical time order. Then write a sentence or two about each picture.

1. _____

_____

2. _____

_____

3. _____

_____

4. _____

_____

IDENTIFYING TIME ORDER

When you write a paragraph, you will often have to organize events according to time. Read the model paragraph and answer the questions.

My Day

I had a terrible day yesterday. First, I woke up an hour late because my alarm clock didn't go off. Then, I was in such a hurry that I burned my hand when I was making breakfast. After breakfast, I got dressed so quickly that I forgot to wear socks. Next, I ran out of the house trying to get the 9:30 bus, but of course I missed it. I wanted to take a taxi, but I didn't have enough money. Finally, I walked the three miles to my office only to discover that it was Sunday! I hope I never have a day as bad as the one I had yesterday.

1. What is the topic sentence?

   _____

2. How are the supporting sentences organized?

   _____

3. What is the concluding sentence?

   _____

USING SIGNAL WORDS

In order to show time relationships, you will need to use signal words to guide the reader from one idea to the next idea. When you write a paragraph using time order, you will need to use these signal words.

first	next	as
second	before	later
then	after	finally

USING PREPOSITIONS OF TIME

It is important to use correct prepositions to show time relationships.

A. Study the prepositions of time and the example. Then draw a circle around the prepositions of time in the model paragraph *My Day*.

Use *at* with specific times: *at* 5:00 / *at* 7:30 / *at* noon / *at* midnight

Use *from* and *to* with a span of time: *from* 6:00 *to* 9:00 / *from* 1941 *to* 1945

Use *in* with other parts of the day:	*in* the afternoon / *in* the morning / *in* the evening (exception: *at* night)
Use *in* with months:	*in* August / *in* June
Use *in* with years:	*in* 1999 / *in* 2001
Use *in* with seasons:	*in* the spring / *in* the summer / *in* the winter
Use *on* with days of the week:	*on* Sunday / *on* Tuesday / *on* Friday
Use *on* with specific dates:	*on* June 30 / *on* April 21, 2001 / *on* New Year's Eve

B. Complete the sentences with the correct prepositions.

1. I lived in Detroit _____ 1995 _____ 1998.

2. Lynn was born _____ 1952.

3. She was born _____ October 31, _____ 4:00 _____ the afternoon.

4. I'll meet you for lunch _____ Tuesday _____ noon.

5. Ruth goes to New York every weekend. She takes the train _____ Saturday _____ 9:00 _____ the morning and arrives in New York _____ 10:45.

ORGANIZING SENTENCES BY TIME

Read the topic sentence. Then read the sentences below it. Together they tell a story. The sentences are not in the correct order. Number them so they follow a logical time order. Put a *1* in front of the sentence that should come first, and so on. Then use all the sentences to write the paragraph.

1. José saved his money and spent two months traveling around the world.

    _____ He spent a week in New York and then flew to London and enjoyed several weeks in Europe.

    _____ When he had seen the sights in Europe, José took a train to Istanbul and visited many places in Asia.

    __1__ First, he flew from his home in Mexico City to New York City.

    _____ After traveling through Asia, he went to South America and finally back home to Mexico.

_____

_____

_____

_____

_____

2. Tim had a hard time keeping his New Year's resolutions.

_____ As the months went on, he broke even more resolutions.

_____ On January 1, he wrote a list of New Year's resolutions.

_____ At the end of January, Tim had broken half of the resolutions.

_____ When the year ended, he realized that he had not kept a single resolution.

_____

_____

_____

_____

_____

3. Mark decided that he wanted to plant a vegetable garden.

_____ At the end of the summer, he picked the vegetables from the garden.

_____ First, he went to a garden store and bought seeds.

_____ Then he went home, prepared the soil, and planted the seeds.

_____ Every day, Mark watered and weeded the garden.

_____

_____

_____

_____

_____

WRITING PARAGRAPHS USING TIME ORDER

1. Dr. Alden is the director of an English language school. Study her schedule for Tuesday, February 21. Write a paragraph about her day. Remember to begin with a topic sentence. Use signal words to guide the reader.

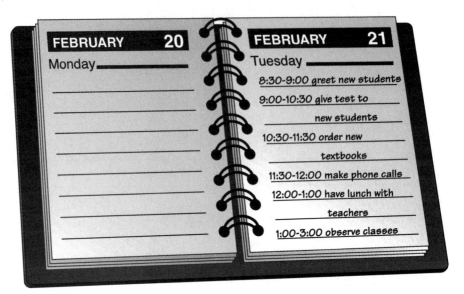

FEBRUARY 20
Monday _____

FEBRUARY 21
Tuesday _____
8:30-9:00 greet new students
9:00-10:30 give test to
   new students
10:30-11:30 order new
   textbooks
11:30-12:00 make phone calls
12:00-1:00 have lunch with
   teachers
1:00-3:00 observe classes

_____
_____
_____
_____
_____
_____

2. Vicki is having a birthday dinner for her friend. She made a list of things she has to do before the party. She put the things on her list in time order. Use her list to write a paragraph about the things she has to do. Remember to begin with a topic sentence. Use signal words to guide the reader.

buy food for dinner at supermarket
pick up birthday cake at bakery
clean house
make dinner
wrap present
set table

_____
_____
_____
_____
_____

3. Babe Ruth was a famous American baseball player. The following time line gives you information about his life. Use the time line to write a paragraph about his life. Remember to begin with a topic sentence. Use signal words to guide the reader.

February 6, 1895:   born in Baltimore, Maryland
1914:   joined the Boston Red Sox
1920:   began to play for the New York Yankees
1921–34:   led the Yankees to seven championships
1936:   elected to the Baseball Hall of Fame

_____

_____

_____

_____

_____

_____

4. Elizabeth Blackwell was the first female medical doctor in the United States. The following time line gives you information about her life. Use the time line to write a paragraph about her life. Remember to begin with a topic sentence. Use signal words to guide the reader.

February 3, 1821:   born in Bristol, England
1832:   emigrated to New York City
1849:   graduated from Geneva Medical School in Geneva, New York
1853:   opened the New York Infirmary because, as a woman, she could not get a job in a hospital
1868:   opened the Women's Medical College of the New York Infirmary
1875:   assisted in founding the London School of Medicine for Women
1910:   died in Hastings, England

_____

_____

_____

_____

_____

_____

_____

_____

_____

You Be the Editor

CAPITALIZATION

Read this report about the history of the computer. All capital letters have been omitted. Correct the paragraph by putting capital letters in the proper places. You will need to add 18 capital letters. Remember these rules of capitalization:

- Use a capital letter for names of people, titles, countries, states, cities, towns, streets, universities, days of the week, months of the year, and holidays.
- Begin the first word of every sentence with a capital letter.
- Begin the first word of a direct quote (what someone says) with a capital letter.
- Capitalize the names of books, magazines, and movies.

throughout history, people have found it necessary to do mathematical computations and keep accounts. in early times, we used groups of sticks or stones to help make calculations. then the abacus was developed in china. these simple methods represent the beginnings of data processing. as computational needs became more complicated, we developed more advanced technologies. one example is the first simple adding machine that blaise pascal developed in france in 1642. another example is the first machine that would do calculations and print out results, which charles babbage designed in england in 1830. in the middle of the twentieth century, researchers at the university of pennsylvania built the first electronic computer. today, of course, we have the computer to perform all kinds of advanced mathematical computations.

On Your Own

Choose a famous person who interests you. Find information about his or her life. Make a time line based on the information and write a paragraph.

CHAPTER 4

Organizing Information by Order of Importance

In Chapter 3, you learned how to organize information according to time order. In this chapter you will learn how to put information in order according to its importance.

Order of Importance

It is often necessary to organize information according to order of importance. You can put the most important piece of information first, or you can save it for last.

RECOGNIZING ORDER OF IMPORTANCE

Read the following model paragraph and answer the questions.

> There are several ways to learn a new language. One way is to spend a lot of time watching television and listening to the radio. Another way is to take classes at a language school or university. The best way to learn a new language is to talk to native speakers.

1. What is the topic sentence?

_____

2. What three ways to learn a new language does the author mention?

_____

_____

_____

3. What does the author feel is the best way?

_____

USING SIGNAL WORDS

Remember to use signal words to guide the reader from one idea to the next idea.

A. Study the list of signal words and phrases for paragraphs using order of importance.

first	second	moreover
first of all	third	most importantly
for one thing	also	for example
one reason that	in addition	finally
the next + *noun*	another + *noun*	the most important + *noun*

B. Read the model paragraph and underline the signal words.

> Bad drivers have several annoying habits. First of all, they change lanes often and don't use their turn signals. In addition, they are rude to other drivers. They get too close to the car in front of them, and they honk their horns. Worst of all, bad drivers ignore the speed limit and drive as fast or slow as they want.

ORDERING IDEAS ACCORDING TO IMPORTANCE

A. In pairs or small groups, discuss this topic: the qualities of a good teacher. Then decide which supporting point is the most important. Put a *1* in front of that point. Decide the next most important point and put a *2* in front of it, and so on.

1. Qualities of a good teacher:

   _____ has knowledge of subject

   _____ cares about students

   _____ has ability to explain clearly

Use the list to complete the paragraph that follows. The topic sentence has been given, but remember to include signal words.

A good teacher has several important qualities. _____

_____

_____

_____

Follow the same steps for the next two topics.

2. Things to consider when choosing a university:

   _____ cost

   _____ location

   _____ quality of education

   _____ size

There are four important things to consider when choosing a university. _____

_____

_____

_____

_____

3. Advantages of marriage:

   _____ having children

   _____ having companionship

   _____ sharing money

   _____ working and making decisions together

Marriage has many advantages. _____

_____

_____

_____

_____

B. **For the next three paragraphs, write your own topic sentence.**

1. Difficult things about living in a foreign country:

   _____ new language

   _____ unfamiliar customs

   _____ different money

   _____ feeling homesick

_____

_____

_____

_____

_____

2. Benefits of a higher education:

_____ have more employment opportunities

_____ earn higher salary

_____ gain prestige

_____ learn valuable information

_____

_____

_____

_____

_____

3. Ways to keep in good shape:

_____ quit smoking

_____ eat healthy foods

_____ exercise daily

_____ get enough sleep

_____

_____

_____

_____

_____

WRITING PARAGRAPHS USING ORDER OF IMPORTANCE

A. Choose one of the following topics to write about.

- things to consider when renting an apartment or buying a house
- advantages of learning a foreign language
- qualities of a good restaurant (or hotel, parent, politician, etc.)
- qualities of a bad restaurant (or hotel, parent, politician, etc.)

B. Make a list of supporting details on the lines provided. Do not worry about the order.

_____   _____

_____   _____

_____   _____

C. Go over your list and cross out any items that do not belong. Then number the supporting ideas in order of their importance. Put a *1* in front of the one you feel is the most important, and so on.

D. Write a topic sentence for your paragraph.

_____

E. Using the topic sentence and your list of supporting points, write a paragraph about your topic. You may begin with what you feel is the most important point or save it for last. Remember to use signal words.

READY TO WRITE

_____

_____

_____

_____

_____

F. Remember that it is very hard to write a perfect paragraph on the first try. Read over your paragraph and look for ways to improve it. Use these questions to help you revise the paragraph you wrote. Rewrite your paragraph.

- Is there a topic sentence?
- Do all the sentences support the topic sentence?
- Are the sentences organized according to order of importance?
- Are there any irrelevant sentences?
- Did you include signal words to guide the reader from one idea to the next?

SMALL GROUP ACTIVITY

A. In small groups, make a list of the advantages of living in a city.

_____   _____

_____   _____

_____   _____

_____   _____

B. Write a paragraph based on your list. Organize your ideas according to the order of their importance. Save the biggest advantage for last.

_____

_____

_____

_____

_____

_____

C. Follow the same procedure with the disadvantages of living in the city.

Equal Order Paragraphs

Sometimes you may feel that all of the points you are using as support are equally important. In this case, you list your points one by one. The order that you use is your choice.

Read the model paragraph. Notice that the author gives equal weight to each point.

There are several things you can do to protect yourself when it gets very hot outside. First of all, you should avoid strenuous activity or wait until the sun goes down. In addition, it is a good idea to wear lightweight and light-colored clothing. It is also important to eat less food and drink more liquids. Finally, try to stay in air-conditioned buildings or go to the beach or the mountains.

1. What is the topic sentence?

   _____

2. How many points does the author discuss? _____

WRITING PARAGRAPHS USING EQUAL ORDER

A. Choose one of the following topics to write about.
- tips for staying healthy
- ways to do well in school
- things I like to do on the weekend

B. Make a list of supporting details on the lines provided. Do not worry about the order.

_____   _____

_____   _____

_____   _____

C. Go over your list and cross out any items that do not belong.

D. Write a topic sentence for your paragraph.

_____

E. Using the topic sentence and your list of supporting points, write a paragraph about your topic. You may put your supporting details in any order you choose. Remember to use signal words.

**READY
TO WRITE**

_____

_____

_____

_____

_____

You Be the Editor

Read the following paragraph. It contains seven mistakes. Find the mistakes and correct them. Then rewrite the corrected paragraph.

Erik enjoy many types of sports. He is liking team sport such as basketball, soccer, and baseball. He also plays traditionals, individual sports like raquetball and golf his favorite sports involve danger as well as exciting. He loves extreme skiing, and skydiving.

On Your Own

Choose one of the other suggested topics from this chapter and write a paragraph about it.

CHAPTER 5

Organizing Information by Space

In this chapter you will learn how to organize information in a paragraph by space order.

Using Space Order

When you describe a place, you use space order to explain where things are located. The easiest way to do this is to choose a starting point. Then you describe where things are located in relation to your starting point. Decide on a logical method to follow. For example, when describing a room, choose a starting point and move clockwise around the room. Other methods are left to right, top to bottom, and back to front.

Read the model paragraph. Choose the picture of the room that the paragraph describes. Put a check below that picture.

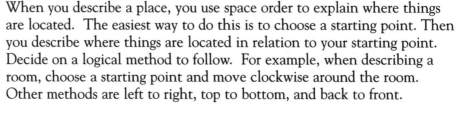

My bedroom is a special place. Like most rooms, it is a rectangle. When you walk in the door, the first thing you notice is the large window on the back wall. It has a beautiful view of the garden. My antique bed is under the window. The left wall is lined with bookcases where I keep my books and pictures. My dresser is on the wall to the right. There is a picture of my parents on the wall above the dresser. In the middle of the room, there is a handmade rug I bought in Mexico.

WRITING TOPIC SENTENCES FOR SPACE ORDER PARAGRAPHS

Write topic sentences for the following paragraphs.

Example

The top of my desk is very well organized. My laptop computer is in the center where it is easy for me to reach. To the left of the computer, I keep a basket with pens, pencils, erasers, and paper clips. My calendar is right next to the basket. There is a small desk lamp in the right corner and a picture of my son next to it. It's very easy for me to work at my desk because everything is always in its place.

1. _____.
In the center of the desk is a pile of old magazines and newspapers. The pile is growing every day. Next to that, there are several dirty coffee cups and a can of soda. There is a lamp in the left corner, but I use it to hold some baseball caps. An old box is on the right side of the desk. Inside the box are my bills and important papers. I also put receipts and letters in the box. The box is getting so full that soon I won't be able to put the top on it.

2. _____.
There are beautiful roses along the fence in front of my house between the street and the driveway. I always put geraniums in my window boxes and pansies under the windows. I also keep a garden behind my house. I have irises, daisies, lilies, and other flowers planted there with a pretty brick path along the edge. I don't have much space left to plant new flowers!

3. _____.
When you walk in the main entrance, the American art is on the first floor on your left. The Asian collection is directly in front of you and the Islamic art is on your right. European paintings and sculptures are on the left side of the museum on the second floor. The Egyptian mummies and statues are on the opposite side of the museum on the second floor. The Greek and Roman statues are on the left side of the third floor. Finally, the African collection is on the right side. It is a big museum with many famous works of art from all over the world.

USING SIGNAL WORDS

The signal words in space order paragraphs are often prepositions of place. Study the following list.

at	in	next to	on the right
at the end	in back of	on	on top of
behind	in front of	on both sides	over
beside	in the center	on the end	under
between	in the middle	on the left	

PRACTICING SPACE ORDER

A. Look at the floor plan of the first floor of Lourie's Department Store. Then read the model paragraph that follows. It is organized by space order. Underline the signal words.

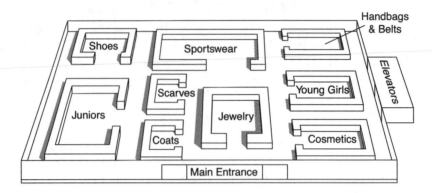

The first floor of Lourie's sells clothing and accessories for women and girls. As you enter the store through the main entrance, the jewelry department is directly in front of you in the middle of the store. The coat department is on the left and the cosmetics department is on the right. The junior shop is on the left, behind coats. Women's shoes are located in the left corner. Next to the shoe department, behind jewelry, is the sportswear department. Handbags and belts are next to sportswear in the right corner. The young girls' department is on the right, between handbags and cosmetics. The elevators are on the right wall.

B. Look at the picture of the jewelry department and complete the following sentences with the correct prepositions.

1. The customers are standing _____ the counter.

2. The jewelry is _____ the case.

3. The little girl is standing _____ her parents.

4. The saleswoman is _____ the counter.

5. There is a mirror _____ the counter.

6. The sale sign is _____ the saleswoman.

WRITING PARAGRAPHS USING SPACE ORDER

A. Complete the floor plan of the second floor of Lourie's using the information in the sentences.

Main Entrance

1. The elevators are on the wall on the right.
2. The men's casual clothing department is in front of the elevators.
3. The coat and suit department is in the middle of the store.
4. Men's shoes are to the left of the coat and suit department.
5. Swimwear is to the left of the entrance.
6. The shirt and tie department is in the left corner, behind the shoe department.

B. Now write a paragraph describing the second floor. Use space order to organize the information. Begin with a topic sentence and use signal words.

The second floor of Lourie's has all the clothing a man needs. _____

_____

_____

_____

_____

_____

_____

**READY
TO WRITE**

C. Write a paragraph describing the third floor based on the following floor plan. Use space order to organize the information. Begin with a topic sentence and use signal words.

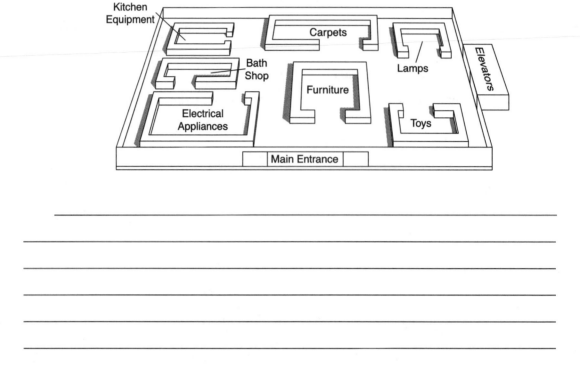

_____

_____

_____

_____

_____

_____

WRITING ABOUT A PLACE

A. Choose one of the following places to write about. Then draw a picture of it. Make a list of some words you need in order to describe things in the space, such as furniture, windows, and clothes.

- your favorite room in your house or apartment
- your closet
- your favorite place to study
- your office or classroom

_____   _____

_____   _____

_____   _____

_____   _____

B. Write a paragraph describing the room. Use space order to organize your information.

**READY
TO WRITE**

_____

_____

_____

_____

_____

_____

C. Ask one of your classmates to read your paragraph and draw a picture of the room based on your description.

D. Compare your picture and your partner's picture of the room. Are there any differences? If yes, discuss them with your partner. Can you think of ways to make your description clearer?

You Be the Editor

Read the following paragraph. It contains five mistakes. Find the mistakes and correct them. Then rewrite the corrected paragraph.

My office is small, but it is comfortably. There are two bigs windows on the left and one small window directly in front of you. my desk fits perfectly under the two big windows. Since my computer is on my desk. I can look out the window as I work. I have a small couch on the wall opposite the desk. Next to the couch, there are a bookcase.

On Your Own

Choose one of the following topics and write a paragraph about it. Use space order to organize your information.

- a doctor's office
- a basic hotel room
- a flower garden
- the view out your window
- your kitchen

_____

_____

_____

_____

_____

_____

_____

CHAPTER 6

The Writing Process

By now you probably understand that writing is a process that involves several steps.

Step One: Prewriting
thinking about your topic and organizing your ideas

Step Two: Writing
using your ideas to write a first draft

Step Three: Revising
improving what you have written

If you follow the steps, and practice by writing often, you will find it easier to write paragraphs and to improve your writing.

Step One: Prewriting

Prewriting is the thinking, talking, reading, and writing you do about your topic before you write a first draft. Prewriting is a way of warming up your brain before you write, just as you warm up your body before you exercise. There are several ways to warm up before you write:

BRAINSTORMING

Brainstorming is a quick way to generate a lot of ideas on a subject. The purpose is to make a list of as many ideas as possible without worrying about how you will use them. Your list can include words, phrases, sentences, or even questions.

To brainstorm, follow these steps:

1. Begin with a broad topic.
2. Write down as many ideas about the topic as you can in 5 minutes.
3. Add more items to your list by answering the questions *what, how, when, where, why,* and *who.*
4. Group similar items on the list together.
5. Cross out items that do not belong.

You can brainstorm ideas by yourself or with a group of people. You already did some brainstorming with your classmates in Chapter 2, when you made a list of ideas about the topic "It is difficult to learn a new language."

BRAINSTORMING ACTIVITY

A. Choose one of the following topics to brainstorm:

- My best friend
- The importance of education
- Good manners
- Money brings _____

B. Write the topic at the top of a piece of paper and follow the steps for brainstorming.

CLUSTERING

Clustering is another prewriting technique. It is a visual way of showing how your ideas are connected using circles and lines. When you cluster, you draw a diagram of your ideas.

To cluster, follow these steps:

1. Write your topic in the center of a blank piece of paper and draw a circle around it.
2. Write any ideas that come into your mind about the topic in circles around the main circle.
3. Connect these ideas to the center word with a line.
4. Think about each of your new ideas, write more related ideas in circles near the new ideas, and then connect them.
5. Repeat this process until you run out of ideas.

Look at the example of a cluster diagram on the topic of television commercials.

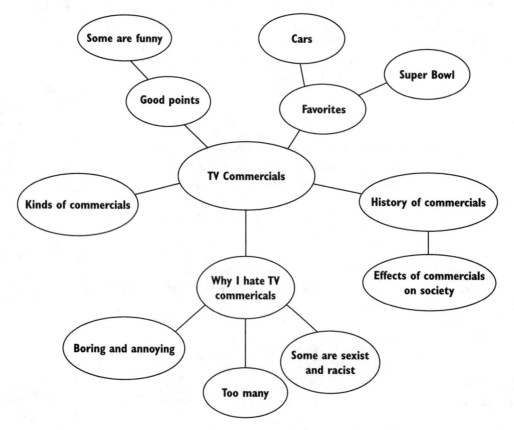

CLUSTERING ACTIVITY

On a separate piece of paper, practice clustering for a paragraph on one of the following topics:

- sports
- music
- gardening
- architecture

Step Two: Writing

After you have spent some time thinking about your topic and doing the necessary prewriting, you are ready for the next step in the writing process: writing your paragraph. When you write the first draft of your paragraph, use the ideas you generated from prewriting as a guide.

As you write, remember to:

- Begin with a topic sentence that states the main idea.
- Include several sentences that support the main idea.
- Stick to the topic—do not include information that does not directly support the main idea.
- Arrange the sentences so that the order of ideas makes sense.
- Use signal words to help the reader understand how the ideas in your paragraph are connected.

WRITING ACTIVITY

Use the ideas you generated in the brainstorming activity or the clustering activity to write a paragraph.

READY
TO WRITE

_____

_____

_____

_____

_____

_____

_____

_____

Step Three: Revising

It is almost impossible to write a perfect paragraph on the first try. The first try is called the first draft. After you complete the first draft, you must look for ways to improve it. This step is called revising. When you revise your paragraph, you can do the following:

- Add new ideas to support the topic
- Cross out sentences that do not support the topic
- Change the order of the sentences.

Use the following checklist to revise your paragraphs.

REVISING CHECKLIST

❏ Make sure you have a topic sentence.
❏ Cross out sentences that do not relate to the main idea.
❏ Check to see if the sentences are in the right order.
❏ Add new ideas if they support the topic sentence.
❏ Make sure you have included signal words to help guide the reader.
❏ Check the punctuation, spelling, and grammar.

REVISING ACTIVITY

Read the paragraph. Think about ways to improve it. Use the revising checklist above to help you. Revise the paragraph and then rewrite it.

My little brother, Tommy, has several annoying habits. For one thing, he follows me everywhere. He is like my shadow. I like my privacy, but because of Tommy I can never be alone. His most annoying habit is eating with his mouth open. It makes me sick just to have lunch with him. I hope he learns some table manners soon. Another problem is that Tommy leaves his toys all over the house. I am always falling over one of his toy cars or trucks. The house is always a mess with Tommy around. Tommy has curly red hair, just like me.

_____

_____

_____

_____

_____

_____

_____

Now find a place in the paragraph to add this sentence.

He even follows me into the bathroom.

PRACTICING THE STEPS OF THE WRITING PROCESS

A. Read the situation and write a paragraph using the steps of the writing process.

> Your friend is having trouble learning English. You are writing him/her a note of encouragement. You want to give some tips about how to learn English.

Prewriting

B. Brainstorm a list (or make a cluster diagram) of ideas about how to learn English.

Writing

C. Write a paragraph that gives advice about how to learn English. Use the information from your prewriting as a guide. Remember to begin with a good topic sentence and to organize your sentences in a logical order.

_____

_____

_____

_____

_____

_____

_____

Revising

D. Read over your paragraph. Think about ways to improve it. Use the revising checklist on page 44 to help you. Revise your paragraph and then rewrite it.

_____

_____

_____

_____

_____

_____

_____

PAIR ACTIVITY

A. Read the situation and write an article. Complete the steps of the writing process with a partner.

> You are writing an article about international students for your local newspaper. You want to include a paragraph about one of your classmates.

Prewriting

B. Make a list of questions that you want to ask your partner.

Here are some suggestions.

- Where are you from?
- What is your native language?
- Have you visited any other countries? What are they?
- Do you know any other languages?
- Are you married or single?
- Do you have any children?
- Why are you learning English?

You might also want to ask questions about your classmate's

- family
- hobbies
- interests
- career or career plans
- education
- travel experiences

C. Talk to your partner and ask him or her the questions you wrote. Write the answers on a piece of paper.

Writing

**READY
TO WRITE**

D. Write the paragraph of the article that describes the person you interviewed. Use the information from your questions as a guide. Remember to begin with a good topic sentence and to group similar ideas about your classmate together.

_____

_____

_____

_____

_____

_____

_____

Revising

E. Now ask your partner to read your paragraph. Does he or she have any suggestions? Write down your partner's suggestions. You can also use the revising checklist on page 44 to help you. Revise your paragraph and then rewrite it.

On Your Own

Choose one of the topics on pages 42 and 43 that you did not already write about. Write a paragraph on the topic. Practice the steps of prewriting (brainstorming or clustering), writing, and revising. Remember to use the revising checklist on page 44.

CHAPTER 7

Supporting the Main Idea

The Main Idea

You have learned that a paragraph has one main idea that is supported with details. Supporting details can come from many places, such as your own personal experience, examples, quotes, or facts.

Using Personal Experience

Writing about a personal experience is one way of supporting a topic sentence. Read the following model paragraph and answer the questions.

Sometimes a stranger can be a real friend. The woman I met on my way home from work yesterday is a great example. I left my office late and forgot that my car needed gas. I had been driving on the expressway for about 10 minutes when the car started making strange noises and then suddenly stopped. I was out of gas, and I was scared because it was getting dark. After a few minutes, a young couple stopped and offered to help me. They went to a gas station, bought a big can of gas, and put the gas in my tank. The woman told me that when she saw me looking so alone and upset, she told her husband to stop. She wanted to help me because she hoped that someone would stop and help her in a similar situation.

1. What is the topic sentence?

   _____

2. How are the supporting sentences organized?

   _____

WRITING ABOUT PERSONAL EXPERIENCES

Prewriting

A. Discuss these expressions with your classmates. What do they mean?

- Money is the root of all evil.
- Two heads are better than one.
- Variety is the spice of life.
- Haste makes waste.
- Don't count your chickens before they hatch.

Writing

B. Choose one expression to write about. Use an experience from your own life to prove or disprove the expression.

_____

_____

_____

_____

_____

_____

Revising

C. Read over the paragraph you wrote. Look for ways to improve it. Use the revising checklist on page 44 to help you. Revise and then rewrite your paragraph.

INDIVIDUAL ACTIVITY

Prewriting

A. Use a personal experience to write a paragraph that supports one of the expressions below. Before you write the paragraph, brainstorm a list of ideas.

- Good things happen when you least expect them.
- Sometimes hard work is not rewarded.
- Things often don't turn out the way you planned.

_____   _____

_____   _____

_____   _____

_____   _____

Writing

B. Now use your list to write the paragraph supporting the expression you chose.

_____

_____

_____

_____

_____

Revising

C. Read over the paragraph you wrote. Look for ways to improve it. Use the revising checklist on page 44 to help you. Revise and then rewrite your paragraph.

Using Facts and Quotes for Support

Good writers often use facts, statistics, or statements from experts to support their topic.

READ AND RESPOND

Read the newspaper article. Underline the facts and statistics that support the main idea.

Fast Food from Asia

Americans used to eating a Big Mac will soon be trying Asian fast food. Thailand's government is planning to open about 1,000 new Thai restaurants in the United States. Many of the new restaurants will be fast-food places called Elephant Jump (the elephant is a traditional symbol of Thailand). These restaurants, which probably would be jointly funded by private investors and the Thai government, would compete with McDonald's, Burger King, Wendy's, and other leading fast-food chains. In addition, Jollibee, a Filipino fast-food chain with restaurants across Asia, recently opened its first U.S. store. Japanese food is hitting the American fast-food market too. Yoshinoya, a Japanese chain specializing in beef and rice dishes, already has over 75 restaurants in North America, and is planning a huge expansion. Yoshinoya reports that by 2006 it hopes to have over 1,000 restaurants outside Japan.

1. What is the main idea of this article?

_____

2. What facts and statistics are used to support the main idea?

_____

_____

_____

WRITING ABOUT INFORMATION IN GRAPHS AND CHARTS

Facts and statistics are often presented in graphs and charts. Sometimes you will need to interpret the information in a graph, chart, or table and use it as support. Here are some words that will help you.

increase	rise	less / fewer
decrease	fall	percent
remain the same	same	percentage

GRAPH AND CHART ACTIVITIES

Student Enrollment

A. Look at the graph below and answer the questions that follow. The name of the graph tells you what kind of information is presented.

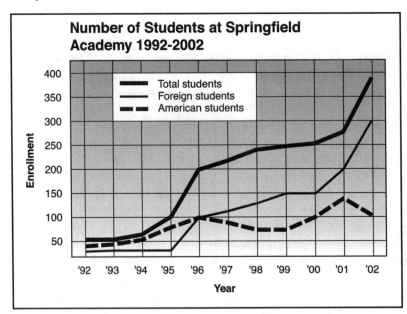

1. In what year was the number of foreign students equal to the number of American students? _____

2. In 1996, how many foreign students attended Springfield Academy?

_____

3. In 2001, how many American students attended Springfield Academy?

_____

4. In what year did the number of American students remain the same?

_____

5. In what years did the number of foreign students remain the same?

_____

6. When did enrollment of foreign students go over 100? _____

7. In what year were there twice as many foreign students as American students?

_____

B. You are a foreign student at Springfield Academy, and you feel that there should be more social and cultural activities for foreign students. Since the number of foreign students is growing every year, you believe that the school has a responsibility to help them socially and culturally as well as academically. Use specific information from the graph to write the part of the paragraph that describes the student body.

Since the number of foreign students at Springfield Academy is growing every year, the school needs to organize more social and cultural activities for us. In the past, this may not have been so important, but today things are different. In 1992,

_____

_____

_____

_____

_____

_____

Because foreign students now represent such a large percentage of the student body, I believe that the school has a responsibility to help us outside the classroom. For example, I would like the school to organize sightseeing tours and arrange visits with American families.

Foreign Student Majors

Prewriting

A. You are opening an English language school. You have to write a report describing the kind of programs you will offer at your school. Look at the chart below and answer the questions. The name of the chart tells you what kind of information is presented.

Percentage Distribution of Foreign Students by Major Fields

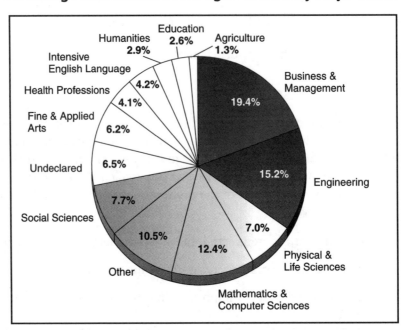

1. What is the most popular field? _____

2. What percentage of all foreign students in the United States are studying engineering? _____

3. What is the second most popular field? _____

4. What percentage are studying business and management? _____

5. This means that almost _____ percent of all foreign students are studying either engineering or business and management.

6. This is followed by _____ percent studying mathematics and computer sciences and _____ percent studying social sciences.

7. What are some other fields that foreign students study? _____
   _____

Writing

B. Based on information in the chart, you feel that the school should have a lot of courses in technical English. Complete the paragraph from the report. Support the topic sentence with facts from the chart.

There is a growing need to provide more technical English programs to foreign students. _____

_____

_____

_____

_____

Revising

C. Read over your paragraph and look for ways to improve it. Use the revising checklist on page 44 to help you. Revise your paragraph and then rewrite it.

The Facts About Running

Prewriting

A. Study the graph and answer the questions.

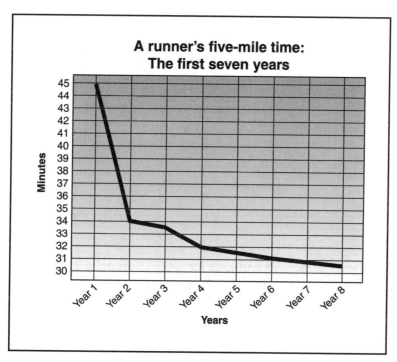

1. What is the name of the graph?

   _____

2. When does the runner achieve the greatest decrease in the amount of time it takes to run five miles (eight kilometers)? _____

3. How long does it take a typical runner to run five miles (eight kilometers) at

   the end of the first year? _____

4. How long does it take at the end of the second year? _____

5. What happens during the following six years? _____

   _____

6. How long does it take during the seventh year? _____

7. How many minutes does the amount of time decrease during the first seven

   year period? _____

Writing

B. You are writing a letter to new members of your running club. Many of the new members are discouraged because it is taking them so long to run five miles. You want to encourage them to continue running. Complete the letter. Support the main idea with facts from the graph.

Dear Members,

   I know that some of you are discouraged because it is taking you so long to run

five miles. But don't give up yet. _____

_____

_____

_____

_____

_____

Revising

C. Read over your paragraph and look for ways to improve it. Use the revising checklist on page 44 to help you. Revise your paragraph and then rewrite it.

Using Quotations for Support

A quotation from an expert on your topic can make your paragraph stronger. Be sure to punctuate the quotes correctly.

RULES FOR PUNCTUATING QUOTES

When you quote someone, follow these rules.
- Put the speaker's exact words inside quotation marks.
- Put a comma after the words that introduce the speaker's words.
- Put periods, commas, or question marks inside the final quotation mark.

Example

The doctor said, "Call me if you don't feel better by Monday."

A. Read the paragraphs and the quotations that follow. Notice that the quotations can be used to support the ideas in the paragraph. Rewrite the paragraphs on a separate piece of paper, adding the quotes where they belong.

1.

Energy Prices and Conservation Rise

The cost of energy is high and continues to rise. People across the country are feeling the effects of the rising costs. As a result, many people are trying to conserve energy at home. They are turning off lights and electrical appliances when they are not using them. People are also trying to use less heat in the winter and use their air conditioners less frequently in the summer. In addition, some Americans are trying to conserve energy on the road. They are buying smaller, more fuel-efficient cars. Many also use public transportation or car pool to save gas. High prices will continue to force people to look for ways to cut back.

a. "Americans spend more than $115 billion each year on fuel and electricity for their homes. On the average, heating and cooling account for about 45% of the energy a home uses. Water heating consumes about 14%, and appliances and other sources about 41%."
(Marianne Watkins, economist.)

b. "Set your thermostats at 75 degrees in the summer and 68 degrees in the winter. This way you will be comfortable and save money and energy."
(Gerald Christopher, director of the Energy Conservation Center.)

2.

Cell Phones and Safety

Talking on a cell phone and driving do not mix. Unfortunately, too many people are combining the two activities and the result could be deadly. In 2000, one survey showed that more than 42 percent of cell phone owners used their phones while driving at least "sometimes." People who talk on the phone and drive often become distracted and do not pay enough attention to driving. They can cause accidents that result in serious injury and death. The 2000 study also reported that the number of people who admitted to talking and driving fell from 82 percent in 1997 to 42 percent in 2000. However, cell phone ownership increased by 150 percent during that time, so there were still more people talking on phones while driving. Among people who reported using cell phones at least sometimes while driving, 87 percent also admitted that it is dangerous to do so. It seems drivers knew that they should pull off the road to make or answer a call, but didn't.

a. "There have been several accidents lately caused by people driving through town talking on cell phones. The drivers were not paying attention to the road. Using cell phones while driving takes a person's eyes and ears off the road." (James Dunn, Elkintown Police Chief)

b. "Drivers should have both hands on the wheel and their attention focused on the road, not on a cell phone conversation. I see more and more patients every week who are in the hospital because of cell phones!" (Joel Weiss, emergency room doctor.)

3.

Cold Winter

Many weather forecasters are predicting that this winter will be colder than usual in the United States. There are many reasons why meteorologists believe this is going to be a long, hard winter. First of all, August was a very cool month. As a result, many parts of Canada never warmed up and the ground is already cold. Secondly, recent studies show that the sun has been putting out less energy for the past two years. Climatologists know that in the past, a decline in solar energy has meant a change to colder weather. Finally, Mexico's El Chicon volcano created a cloud of dust and acid. This is shielding the earth from sunlight.

a. "This is troubling because even a small reduction of solar energy can affect agriculture worldwide." (Stephen Schneider)

b. "There are twenty-two volcanoes around the globe sending tons of sulphur dioxide into the atmosphere. The sulphur dioxide just sits there and blocks sunlight." (Reid Bryson)

You Be the Editor

Read the following magazine article about dieting. It contains seven mistakes. Find the mistakes and correct them. Then rewrite the corrected article.

Do Diets Work?

Doctors and dieters agree that is possible to lose weight by dieting. The difficulty part, they report, is keeping the weight of after you to lose it.

Research indicates that many people successfully lose weight at some point in life, but most people gain the weight back within three years. Ian Fenn is a doctor who specializes in weight problems. He says that there is many sorts of diets, and medical science is working to figure out how to control body weight. "It is also a matter", he says, "of getting people to change their lifestyles. Each person need to find the right combination of diet and exercise."

On Your Own

1. Look through newspapers and magazines for a chart or graph that interests you. Make a copy or cut it out of the newspaper or magazine. Write a paragraph explaining the information in the chart or graph.

2. With a partner, make up your own information for a chart or graph on a topic of interest to you. Then write a paragraph interpreting the data.

CHAPTER 8

Giving Instructions

When you explain the step-by-step process of how to do or make something, you are giving instructions. In this chapter you will learn how to write instructions that are clear and easy to follow. When you write instructions or directions, you need to use time order, and sometimes space order.

Recognizing Processes

Read the following model paragraph and answer the questions.

How to Pack a Suitcase

Most people hate to pack, but following these steps helps make packing easy. First, put all the items you want to take on your bed and organize everything into groups. For example, put all your shoes in one group, all your clothes in another, all your toiletries in a third, and so on. Second, put your toiletries in plastic bags and your shoes in shoe bags. After that, place your shoes on the bottom of the suitcase. Then take your pants, fold them in half, and roll them up. Once rolled, place them in the bottom of the suitcase around the shoes. Fill empty space on the bottom with socks and underwear. Next, fold and put flat items, such as shirts and sweaters, as a second layer. Put your bags of toiletries between layers of clothes. Finally, place your last layer of items in the suitcase so that there are no spaces left between items. This way of packing helps you get organized and stay organized when you travel.

1. What is the topic sentence?

   _____

2. What steps does the author give?

   _____   _____

   _____   _____

   _____   _____

3. How are the steps organized?

   _____

Writing Topic Sentences for Process Paragraphs

The topic sentence of a process paragraph must identify the process and tell something about it. Write a topic sentence for the following paragraphs.

Example

There are several steps you must follow to get your student identification card.

First, get a copy of the receipt that shows you paid your tuition. Then take the receipt to the Student Affairs Building. Go to the ID office and show the secretary your receipt. After that, get your picture taken. Remember to smile! Wait three minutes for your picture to be processed and your ID to be printed. Finally, sign your ID card and put it in your wallet.

1. _____

   _____

First of all, write your name and address in the upper left hand corner of the envelope. Then write the name and address of the person you are mailing the letter to in the center of the envelope. This usually takes three lines. Put the name on the first line. Write the street address on the second line and the city and state on the third line. Remember to include the zip code. Finally, put a stamp in the upper right hand corner. The most important thing to remember is to write neatly!

2. _____

   _____

First, fill a clean vase with water. Second, cut most of the flowers and greens so they are approximately two times the height of your vase. Then, cut a couple of the flowers two inches longer. After you are finished cutting the flowers, you can begin to put the greens in the vase. Now add the other flowers. Start at the outer edge of your vase. Put the longest flowers in the center of your arrangement. Then take a few steps back and admire your bouquet.

3. _____

   _____

It is a good idea to practice tying a bow tie by putting the tie around your leg just above your knee. Begin by holding one end of the tie in each hand. Close your eyes. Then, pretend that you are tying your shoelaces. When you open your eyes, you will see that you have made a bow. Adjust the tie so it looks like a nice bow tie. When you feel you are ready, try tying a bow tie on your neck.

USING SIGNAL WORDS

When you describe a process you put the steps in time order. In order to make the steps clear, you should use time order signal words to guide the reader from one step to the next. Review the signal words on page 28. Complete the following paragraph about how to make popcorn. Use the correct signal words.

It is very easy to make good popcorn. _____First_____, put three tablespoons of oil in a large heavy pot. _____, heat the oil on a high flame until one kernel of popcorn pops when you drop it into the hot oil. When the oil is hot enough, pour one-quarter cup of popcorn into the pot and cover it with a lid. _____, reduce the flame to medium and begin to shake the pot gently. Continue shaking the pot until all the corn has popped. _____, empty the popcorn into a large bowl and add melted butter and salt.

RECOGNIZING THE ORDER OF INSTRUCTIONS

Making a Sundae

A. The following sentences describe how to make a chocolate sundae, but they are not in the correct time order. Find the topic sentence and put a 1 in front of it. Use the signal words to help you put the steps in the right order.

_____ Next, cover with whipped cream.

_____ Chocolate sundaes are one of the easiest desserts to make.

_____ Finally, sprinkle chopped nuts on the whipped cream and put a cherry on top.

_____ Then pour two tablespoons of hot fudge sauce over the ice cream.

_____ First, put one scoop of your favorite kind of ice cream in a dish.

B. Now write the ordered steps in paragraph form.

_____

_____

_____

_____

_____

_____

_____

_____

The Heimlich Maneuver

A. The following sentences describe what to do if someone is choking. First, find the topic sentence. Then put the sentences in the right order.

_____ Then make a fist with one hand and grasp the fist with your other hand. Put your hands just below his rib cage.

_____ The Heimlich maneuver is a method that anyone can use to help someone who is choking on a piece of food.

_____ Finally, press your fist into the victim's abdomen with a quick upward movement

_____ The first thing you should do is stand behind the choking person and put your arms around his waist.

_____ If the person is still choking, you may need to repeat the maneuver.

B. Now write a paragraph based on the steps.

_____

_____

_____

_____

_____

_____

_____

_____

_____

READY TO WRITE

Potting a Plant

A. Study the pictures. They show how to pot a plant. Use the pictures to number the steps following in the correct time order.

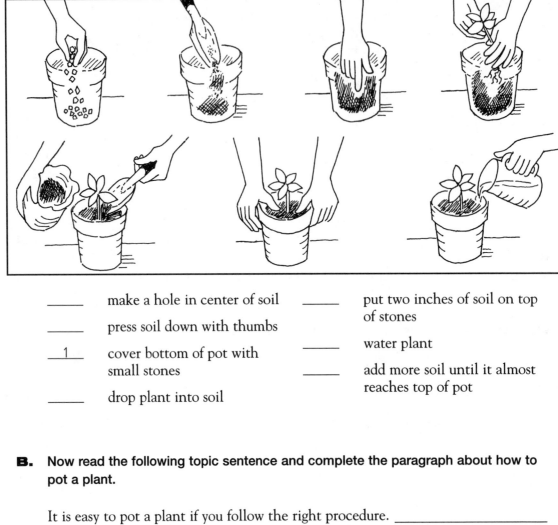

_____ make a hole in center of soil

_____ press soil down with thumbs

__1__ cover bottom of pot with small stones

_____ drop plant into soil

_____ put two inches of soil on top of stones

_____ water plant

_____ add more soil until it almost reaches top of pot

B. Now read the following topic sentence and complete the paragraph about how to pot a plant.

It is easy to pot a plant if you follow the right procedure. _____

_____

_____

_____

_____

_____

_____

_____

Writing a Process Paragraph

Choose one of the following processes to write about.

How to:
- plan a party
- make your favorite dish
- change a flat tire
- study for an exam
- make your bed
- plant a garden

Prewriting

A. Make a list of all the steps in the process.

_____   _____

_____   _____

_____   _____

B. Number the steps so they are in the correct time order.

Writing

C. Write a paragraph describing the process. Use the list of steps from your prewriting as a guide. Be sure to write a topic sentence that clearly states the process that you are describing.

READY TO WRITE

_____

_____

_____

_____

_____

_____

_____

_____

_____

Revising

D. Read over your paragraph and look for ways to improve it. Use the revising checklist on page 44 to help you. Revise your paragraph and then rewrite it.

DESCRIBING THE STEPS IN AN EXPERIMENT

Processes are very important in scientific and technical fields.

A. Study the following lab report.

WATER EXPANSION EXPERIMENT
Purpose: To show that water expands when frozen
Materials: A glass jar
Procedure:
1. Fill the glass jar halfway with water.
2. Mark the outside of the jar at water level.
3. Put the jar in the freezer until the water freezes.
4. Observe the new water level.
Results: The level of the frozen water is higher.

B. Now read the following model paragraph that describes the process of the experiment. Then answer the questions.

You can do a simple experiment to prove that water expands when it is frozen. All you need is an empty glass jar. First, fill half the jar with water. Then mark the water level on the outside of the jar. After that, put the jar in a freezer until the water freezes. When the water is frozen, take the jar out of the freezer and observe the new water level. You will see that the level of the frozen water is higher. This proves that water expands when it is frozen.

1. What is the topic sentence? _____

_____

2. What signal words are used in the paragraph? _____

_____

3. How many steps are described? _____

WRITING ABOUT AN EXPERIMENT

Prewriting

A. Read the following lab report. Discuss it with a classmate.

SOLAR ENERGY EXPERIMENT

Purpose: To show that black is a better collector of solar energy
than white

Materials: 2 tin cans, black and white paint, room thermometer

Procedure:

1. Paint the cans—one black, one white.

2. Fill the cans with water.

3. Put the cans in direct sunlight for three hours.

4. Check the temperature of the water in the cans and compare.

Results: The water in the black can is hotter.

Writing

B. Now use the information to write a paragraph describing the process of the experiment. Remember to begin with a topic sentence and use signal words.

**READY
TO WRITE**

_____

_____

_____

_____

_____

_____

Revising

C. Read over your paragraph and look for ways to improve it. Use the revising checklist on page 44 to help you. Revise your paragraph and then rewrite it.

USING TIME ORDER AND SPACE ORDER TO GIVE DIRECTIONS

When you explain to someone how to get to a specific place, you are giving directions. In order to make your directions clear, you need to use both time order and space order.

A. Study this list of useful words for writing directions.

continue	across the street from _____
go as far as _____	between _____ and _____
go north (or south, east, west)	in the middle
go one block (or two blocks, etc.)	next door to
go past _____	on the corner
go straight (until you come to _____)	on the left (or the right)
turn left (or right)	on the left side (or the right side)

B. Look carefully at the map of the historical area of Philadelphia. Find the Visitor Center on the map. Where is it located?

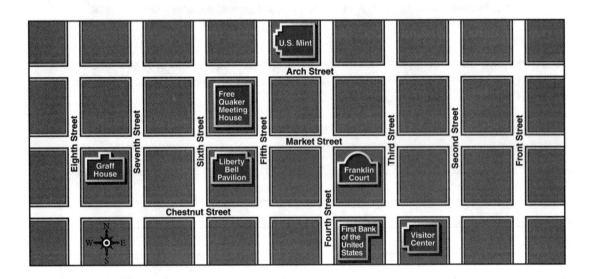

C. Read these model directions:

> In order to get from the Visitor Center to the U.S. Mint, follow these directions. First, go north two blocks from the Visitor Center. Then turn left on Arch Street. Continue two blocks on Arch Street to 5th Street. The U.S. Mint is on your right.

D. You work at the Visitor Center. Write directions from the Visitor Center to each of the following places for a tour guidebook.

1. Liberty Bell

_____

_____

_____

_____

_____

2. Free Quaker Meeting House

_____

_____

_____

_____

_____

3. First Bank of the United States

_____

_____

_____

_____

_____

4. Franklin Court

_____

_____

_____

_____

_____

5. Graff House

_____

_____

_____

_____

_____

You Be the Editor

Read the following paragraph. It contains nine mistakes. Find the errors and correct them. Then rewrite the corrected paragraph.

It is not difficult to remove the shell from a lobster if you follow these step. First, you should to put the lobster on it's back and remove the two large claws and tail section. After that, You must also twist off the flippers at end of tail section. After these are twisted off, use you fingers to push the lobster meat out of the tail in one piece. Next, remove the black vein. From the tail meat. Finally, before you sit down to enjoy your meal, break open the claws with a nutcracker and remove the meat.

On Your Own

1. Draw a simple map of your neighborhood. Label the streets and important buildings. Practice the vocabulary of giving directions by writing directions from your house to several other places. Check your directions by having another student follow them.

2. Write a paragraph that tells how to protect yourself when a hurricane, blizzard, tornado, or other natural disaster is forecast for your area.

3. Write a paragraph that describes the steps involved in getting your driver's license.

CHAPTER 9

Writing Descriptions

Writing a description is like creating a picture using words. The key to writing a good description is using specific details that create exactly the picture you want.

Describing People

Read the model paragraph and answer the question that follows.

The police are looking for a woman who stole a diamond necklace from Dayton's Jewelry Store. According to the store manager, the woman is approximately five feet tall, very thin, light-skinned, and about 60 years old. She has short, straight gray hair and wears glasses. Her most distinguishing mark is the dimple in her chin. When she was last seen, she was wearing heavy blue eye make-up and large, silver hoop earrings. She had on a short black coat and black pants. If you see anyone fitting this description, contact the police deparment immediately.

What details does the author use to describe the woman?

_____   _____

_____   _____

_____   _____

USING DESCRIPTIVE WORDS

When you write a description you should use words that relate to the senses of sight, sound, touch, smell, and taste. These are called sensory words. Sensory words help the reader imagine what you are describing.

WORDS FOR DESCRIBING PEOPLE

When you describe what a person looks like, you write about physical characteristics such as height, weight, and hair color. Again, the key to writing a good description is to use details that help the reader imagine the person you are describing. Here are some words that can help you describe people.

Height	Body type	Hair	Features
medium	athletic	blonde	beard
short	heavy	brunette	dimple
tall	muscular	curly	freckles
	petite	dark	glasses
	plump	light	mole
	skinny	long	mustache
	stocky	red	scar
	thin	short	wrinkles
		straight	
		wavy	

WRITING A DESCRIPTION OF A PERSON

Prewriting

A. Read this telephone conversation.

Lucia: I'm so glad you called. I have a big problem and I hope you can help me.

Clara: What's the problem? I'll help if I can.

Lucia: My cousin is coming home tonight from his trip to Europe and I'm supposed to pick him up at the airport at seven o'clock. The problem is that I just found out I have to work late tonight. Can you possibly pick him up for me?

Clara: Sure. What airline is he taking?

Lucia: British Airways. Flight 179.

Clara: OK. But how will I recognize him?

Lucia: Well, he's medium height and average weight. He wears glasses, and he dresses very well.

Clara: That could be almost anyone. Can you be more specific?

Lucia: Well, his hair is blonde and curly. I almost forgot! He has a beard.

Clara: What's his name?

Lucia: Ernie Norton.

Clara: OK, no problem. I'll find him.

Lucia: Thank you so much!

At the last minute, Clara is unable to go to the airport. Her brother Tim has agreed to pick Ernie up instead. Clara is writing a note to Tim describing Ernie so that he will be able to find him. What should Clara's note say? The following questions will help you.

- Is he tall or short?
- Is he fat or thin?
- What color hair does he have?
- Is his hair curly or straight?
- Does he wear glasses?
- Is there anything about him that you notice immediately?

Writing

B. Pretend you are Clara. Write a note to Tim describing Ernie.

Dear Tim,

_____

_____

_____

_____

_____

Revising

C. Read over your note and make sure you have added enough details. Revise your note and then rewrite it.

INDIVIDUAL ACTIVITY

Prewriting

A. Choose a member of your family to describe. Make a list of descriptive details.

_____   _____

_____   _____

_____   _____

Writing

B. Using your list as a guide, write a description of your relative. Remember to include descriptive words from page 70.

_____

_____

_____

_____

_____

_____

_____

Revising

C. Read over your description and make sure you have a topic sentence and enough descriptive detail. You can also use the revising checklist on page 44 to help you. Revise your description and then rewrite it.

CLASS ACTIVITY

A. Choose someone in your class to describe.

B. Write a short description of that person, but do not mention his or her name. Remember to include details about size, hair color, distinguishing marks, and so on. Write your description on a separate piece of paper.

C. Give the description to your teacher. The teacher will give each student one of the descriptions. Read the description you were given. Can you guess who it is?

On Your Own

Write a description of one of the boys in this picture. You might need to review some vocabulary with your teacher.

Describing Objects

When you describe things, or objects, you also want to create a picture with words.

WORDS FOR DESCRIBING OBJECTS

Here are some words you can use to describe objects.

Color	Texture	Shape
black	rough	oval
orange	sharp	rectangular
purple	silky	round
yellow	smooth	square

Size	Smell	Taste
average	fresh	bitter
big	fruity	bland
huge	pungent	fruity
small	smokey	nutty
	strong	salty
		sour
		spicy
		sweet

Read the model paragraph and answer the question that follows.

   I found the perfect pocket watch in an antique store to give my son for his 21st birthday. The face of the watch is white. It measures about one and one half inches (4 centimeters) in diameter. The numbers on the face are nice and big and the blue hands are very long and thin. The back of the watch is gold with three letters engraved on it. They are probably the original owner's initials. The watch came with a chain that is about 12 inches (30 centimeters) long. The best thing about the watch is that it stills keeps perfect time after all these years.

What details does the author use to describe the pocket watch?

_____   _____

_____   _____

_____   _____

DESCRIBING PRODUCTS

A. You work in the advertising division of Lourie's Department Store. You are working on the holiday mail-order catalog. You have just completed the first page. Reread your product descriptions.

1. Keep warm this winter with this practical but good-looking plaid blanket. It is 52 inches (132 cm) wide and 76 inches (193 cm) long, with fringe on two sides. It is handmade in England of the finest-quality wool. $100. Item A31.

2. Be on time with these accurate and elegant Swiss watches. Both the man's and the woman's have black leather bands and gold faces. The face of the man's watch is 1 1/4 inches (3 cm) and the face of the woman's is 3/4 inches (2 cm). Both watches have a one-year guarantee. $280. Item D12.

3. You'll love this soft cashmere sweater. It has long sleeves, a soft collar and five pearl buttons down the front. It comes in four colors: black, white, red, blue. It is available in sizes small, medium, and large. $99. Item A17.

4. This beautiful, antique Chinese vase makes a perfect gift. It is 18 inches (46 cm) tall and comes with a wooden stand. It has two handles and is available in blue or white. $200. Item B5.

B. Now write short descriptions of these items for the next page of the catalog. Use your imagination. Remember, when you describe an object, you will need to mention such things as shape, size, color, and texture.

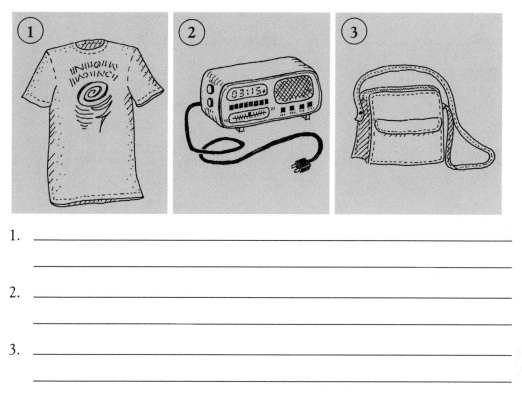

1. _____
   _____

2. _____
   _____

3. _____
   _____

WRITING A DESCRIPTION OF A BUILDING

Prewriting

A. Draw a picture of a special building in your hometown. Then make a list of important details about the building.

```
┌─────────────────────────────────────────────┐
│                                               │
│                                               │
│                                               │
│                                               │
│                                               │
│                                               │
│                                               │
│                                               │
└─────────────────────────────────────────────┘
```

_____   _____

_____   _____

_____   _____

Writing

READY TO WRITE

B. Write a description of the building. Use the list from your prewriting as a guide.

_____

_____

_____

_____

_____

C. Give your description to a classmate and ask him or her to draw the building using your description.

Revising

D. Compare the picture to the description. How are they alike? What are the differences? The differences should give you clues to help you revise your paragraph. Revise your paragraph and then rewrite it.

Describing Places

A. Read the following postcard that Carolyn wrote to her friend Sharon.

Hi,

    I'm sorry I didn't get to see you while you were in Boston. It was so hot here that we went to our favorite campsite in the mountains. The site is very clean and rarely crowded. It's near the top of Mount Greylock, in the Berkshires. The trails are long and shady. From the tower at the top of the mountain you can look at the valleys and rivers below. The view is spectacular in the evening. The sky turns bright orange and pink as the sun sets behind the hills. Best of all, there's always a nice cool breeze! Let me know when you'll be in Boston again.

                Love, Carolyn

Sharon Laroche
84 Maple Street
Hawthorne, NY 10532

What details does the author use to describe Mount Greylock?

_____   _____

_____   _____

_____   _____

B. Read the list of words that can be used to describe places.

clean	hilly	old
cold	hot	quiet
colorful	humid	rural
cool	industrial	sandy
crowded	modern	spectacular
dirty	mountainous	wide
flat	narrow	windy

C. Look at the picture of Elephant Rock Beach. Pretend you are on vacation there and write a postcard to a friend describing it. Use at least nine descriptive words. Underline the descriptive words you use.

PAIR ACTIVITY

In this activity you will write a description of the hometown of one of your classmates. If everyone is from the same place, ask your partner questions about another city he or she has visited. Follow these steps.

Prewriting

A. Talk to your partner about his or her hometown. Make a list of questions to ask your partner.

Here are some suggestions.

- What is the name of your hometown?
- Where is it located?
- What size is it?
- How many people live there?
- What is the weather like?
- What is the most impressive thing about your hometown?

You might also want to ask questions about

- history
- geography
- architecture
- services
- entertainment
- famous people who have lived there

B. Copy your questions on a separate piece of paper. Leave enough space to write in your partner's answers. Ask your partner the questions you prepared.

Writing

READY TO WRITE

C. Use the information you have about your partner's hometown to write a paragraph. Be sure to give the name of the place in the topic sentence.

_____

_____

_____

_____

_____

Revising

D. Now ask your partner to read your paragraph. Does he or she have any suggestions? Revise your paragraph based on your partner's suggestions. You can also use the revising checklist on page 44 to help you. Revise your paragraph and then rewrite it.

INDIVIDUAL ACTIVITY

Think about your favorite place to go and relax. Is it a beach? Your bedroom? A coffee shop?

Prewriting

A. Brainstorm a list of details describing the place.

_____   _____

_____   _____

_____   _____

Writing

B. Use your list to write a paragraph.

_____

_____

_____

_____

_____

_____

READY TO WRITE

Revising

C. Read over your description. Did you include enough specific details about the place? What else can you include to make your description clearer? Use the revising checklist on page 44 to help you. Revise your paragraph and then rewrite it.

You Be the Editor

Read the following description of a missing dog. It contains six mistakes. Find the mistakes and correct them. Then rewrite the corrected paragraph.

My dog, Bette, is missing. She is a small black poodle with browns eyes. her hair is short and curly. Bette weighs 8 pounds and is about one and a half foots long. She has a short tail, long, floppy ears, and small feet. She is wear a silver collar with an ID tag on it. She is very friendly around people and love children. I have had Bette for 6 years, since she was a puppy, and I miss her very much. I am offering a $50 reward for anyone which finds Bette. Please call me at 305-892-7671.

On Your Own

Imagine you are one of the *paparazzi*—photographers who follow famous people and take their pictures. You have just taken a good photo of a famous person and you contact a magazine to try to sell your photo. Name the person and describe the photograph. What does he or she look like in the picture? What is he or she wearing? What other things or people are in the picture? (If you cannot imagine a photo, look for one in a magazine or newspaper and describe it.)

Example

I have a photograph of Prince William. He is walking on a London street. He is wearing sunglasses and a gray raincoat. He has a new hairstyle, and he is holding hands with a beautiful lady. She looks much older than the prince! They are both carrying small shopping bags with the name of a famous jeweler on them.

CHAPTER 10

Expressing an Opinion

Opinion

When you write, it is often necessary to state your opinion about something you believe to be true.

A. Read the article below and the two opinion paragraphs. Answer the questions that follow.

> The number of children in public schools in the United States who speak little or no English is increasing rapidly. For example, students in the Washington, DC, school system speak 127 different languages and dialects. In the California public schools, one out of six students was born outside the United States, and one out of three speaks a language other than English at home. These students and their teachers face many challenges, including what language to use in the classroom. Some people believe children of immigrants should be taught in their native language. Others believe that these children should be taught in English only.

1.   In my opinion, children of immigrants should be taught in their native language. First of all, these children will feel more comfortable in a strange school if they hear and speak their native language. In addition, they will be able to understand subjects like math, history, and science more easily if they are taught in their native language and do not have to struggle with the new language. Finally, students who use their native language in school are better able to keep their cultural identity.

a. What is the author's opinion?

_____

_____

b. What three reasons does the author give to support his or her opinion?

_____

_____

_____

2.   In my opinion, children of immigrants should be taught in English. First, they will learn the new language more quickly if all their subjects are taught in English. Second, children of immigrants will feel less isolated if they are taught in the same language as the rest of the children. Finally, they will be able to perform better on standardized tests if they have learned the material in their classes in English.

a. What is the author's opinion?

_____

_____

b. What three reasons does the author give to support his or her opinion?

_____

_____

_____

STATING YOUR OPINION

Read the following sentences. Circle the word or phrase in parentheses that you think best expresses your opinion.

Example

It is _____ for mothers with small children to work outside of the house. (*(good)*/ *harmful*)

1. Smoking _____ be banned in restaurants. (*should* / *should not*)

2. Nuclear energy _____ the best way to meet our energy needs. (*is* / *is not*)

3. Women _____ be required to serve in the army. (*should* / *should not*)

4. Prayer _____ be allowed in the public schools. (*should* / *should not*)

5. It _____ acceptable to use animals for laboratory experiments. (*is* / *is not*)

6. The drinking age _____ be lowered to age 18. (*should* / *should not*)

7. Governments _____ use the death penalty to punish criminals. (*should / should not*)

8. _____ is the most exciting sport. (*Hockey / Soccer / Tennis*)

9. Modern architecture _____ ugly. (*is / is not*)

10. UFOs (unidentified flying objects) _____ exist. (*do / do not*)

WRITING TOPIC SENTENCES THAT STATE YOUR OPINION

The following useful phrases are often used to introduce opinions that serve as topic sentences.

> I believe (that)   I think (that)
>
> In my opinion,   I feel (that)

Write an opinion topic sentence for each of the statements in the previous activity.

Example

> In my opinion, it is good for mothers with small children to work outside of
>
> of the house.

1. _____

2. _____

3. _____

4. _____

5. _____

6. _____

7. _____

8. _____

9. _____

10. _____

SUPPORTING YOUR OPINION

In the body of the paragraph, you will give reasons, examples, or facts to support your opinion. It is helpful to list your reasons in order of importance. The following phrases are often used as signal words to introduce facts, reasons, and examples.

First of all,	Moreover,
For one thing,	For example,
One reason that	Secondly,
Also,	Thirdly,
In addition,	Finally,

Choose three of your opinions and give two or three reasons, examples, or facts to support each one.

Example

Opinion: **In my opinion**, it is good for mothers with small children to work outside of the house.

Reason 1: A working mother can help pay for the many things the children need.

Reason 2: A working mother is a good role model for her children, especially her daughters.

Reason 3: Children who have caregivers other than their mothers learn better social skills.

1. Opinion: _____

   Reason 1: _____

   Reason 2: _____

   Reason 3: _____

2. Opinion: _____

   Reason 1: _____

   Reason 2: _____

   Reason 3: _____

3. Opinion _____

   Reason 1 _____

   Reason 2 _____

   Reason 3 _____

WRITING AN OPINION PARAGRAPH

Prewriting

A. Look at the opinions and reasons you wrote in the last exercise. Choose one of your opinions as the topic for a paragraph.

Writing

B. Write a paragraph. Use your opinion as the topic sentence. Then use your reasons to write supporting sentences. Remember to use signal words.

_____

_____

_____

_____

_____

_____

_____

READY TO WRITE

Revising

C. Read over your paragraph and look for ways to improve it. Use the following questions below to help you. Revise your paragraph and then rewrite it.

- Does the topic sentence state your opinion?
- Do you have two or three reasons to support your opinion?
- Have you used signal words to introduce your reasons?
- Are there any irrelevant sentences?

PAIR ACTIVITY

Prewriting

A. Discuss the following list of sentences about children and TV with a partner. Some of the sentences support the opinion that TV is good for children. Other sentences support the opinion that TV is bad for children.

1. TV exposes children to different countries, cultures, and ideas.
2. Children can learn about science, history, and the arts.
3. There is too much violence on TV.
4. Children see a false picture of human relationships.
5. Educational programs teach children basic skills such as reading and writing.
6. Watching TV is too passive. Children should be doing more creative and active things.
7. Children want to buy everything they see on commercials.
8. TV can be harmful to children's eyes.
9. News programs inform children about what is going on in their community.
10. TV gives children free and interesting entertainment.

B. With your partner, divide the list into two groups.

TV is good for children	TV is bad for children
_____	_____
_____	_____
_____	_____
_____	_____
_____	_____
_____	_____

Writing

C. You are concerned parents. The principal of your child's school asked you to write an article about children and television for the school newsletter. What is your opinion? Is TV good or bad for children? Choose an opinion with your partner, then use your opinion as the topic sentence for your paragraph. Use the list of reasons in B as supporting sentences. Add any other reasons you can think of to support your opinion.

_____

_____

_____

_____

_____

_____

_____

_____

Revising

D. Revise your paragraph on a separate piece of paper by adding two of the following sentences. Be sure to choose the ones that support your opinion and put them in a logical place. Revise your paragraph and then rewrite it.

- There are over seven acts of violence per hour on prime-time TV.
- The most violent TV shows are on Saturday mornings, when many children are watching.
- When children see something on TV, they become interested and want to learn more about it.
- Children learn to recognize famous people.
- News programs teach children about important things that are going on in the world.

Prewriting

A. Read the letter and answer the questions that follow.

> Dear Editor:
>
> Last month our nine-year-old daughter was hit by a car. The man driving the car was drunk at the time and didn't stop at a stop sign. Our little girl was in the hospital for three long weeks. My husband and I didn't know if she would live or die. It was a terrible time for us. Although today she is alive, we are afraid something like that might happen again.
>
> Recently we heard that the punishment for the driver was only a $500 fine. He didn't go to jail and he didn't lose his license. Today he is free to drive and possibly commit the same crime again. Maybe next time he will kill somebody.
>
> We feel the laws against drinking and driving should be very strict. Drunk drivers should pay for their crimes. We think their licenses should be taken away. We need stricter laws!
>
> Yours truly,
>
> *Kathleen Johnson*
>
> Kathleen Johnson
> Philadelphia, PA

1. Do you think drinking and driving is a serious crime? _____

2. Which of the following do you think is a fair punishment for drinking and driving? Why?

    _____ lose license   _____ lose car

    _____ get jail sentence   _____ pay fine of $500 or more

Writing

B. Write a paragraph that expresses your opinion about drinking and driving.

_____

_____

_____

_____

_____

_____

_____

Revising

C. Read your paragraph again. Do all your sentences support your opinion? Are all your reasons clear? Revise your paragraph and then rewrite it. This time include one of the following facts:

- A U.S. Department of Transportation study found that drinking by drivers causes 25,000 deaths per year.
- Each year over 20 percent of all traffic fatalities in the United States are caused by drunk drivers.

SMALL GROUP ACTIVITIES

Read and Respond

Prewriting

A. Read this news article and study the police report. In small groups, discuss the situation and the three suspects. Together, decide who you think committed the crime.

Computer Crime Hits Local Bank

NATIONAL CITY BANK and Trust Company is the largest bank in the city. Its assets are in the billions of dollars. In 1960 the bank computerized its operations. The bank had considered itself very lucky because it had not been troubled by computer crime—until last week. On Wednesday, the accountants discovered that a total of $400,000 was missing from several different accounts. It is not yet known where the funds were transferred. Police investigation has led to three possible suspects. These three people had easy access to the computer system that transferred the funds out of the bank.

POLICE REPORT

(a) **Norman Glass**—Computer operator

    – has worked for bank six months

    – earns low salary

    – has wife and four children

    – lives in large house and drives expensive new car

    – before working at bank he served five years in army
      (won a Medal of Honor)

(b) **Richard Allen**—Vice president of bank

    – has been with bank 35 years

    – has a good history with bank

    – recently lost a lot of money in stock market

    – takes expensive vacations

    – earns very high salary

(c) **Jim Tomlin**—Computer consultant

    – has worked for bank two years

    – is active in church and community

    – graduated top of his class at Harvard

    – supports widowed mother who is sick and lives in
      expensive nursing home

    – has a gambling problem

Writing

B. Write a paragraph stating your opinion about who you think committed the crime. Be sure to give specific reasons to support your opinion.

READY
TO WRITE

_____

_____

_____

_____

_____

_____

_____

Revising

C. Read over your paragraph and look for ways to improve it. Use the revising checklist on page 44 to help you. Revise your paragraph and then rewrite it.

Giving Advice

READY TO WRITE

A. If you were the advice consultant for your newspaper, how would you respond to the following letters? Respond to each one with your opinion. Then share your responses with your classmates.

1.

> Dear Adviser:
>
> My mother-in-law drives me crazy. She finds fault with everything I do. She thinks I don't take good enough care of my family. She criticizes my cooking and my housekeeping as well as the way I handle the children. My husband says I should just ignore her, but that is difficult because she lives across the street. What do you think I should do?
>
> Mrs. S.L.

Dear Mrs. S.L.:

_____

_____

_____

_____

_____

_____

_____

The Adviser

2.

Dear Adviser:

My friend and I are having a terrible argument and we hope you can settle it for us. I say it's okay for girls to call boys on the telephone. I say it is all right for a girl to let a guy know she likes him and would like to go out with him. My friend disagrees. She says that guys still prefer to do the courting, but girls make it difficult now because they are so aggressive. She says guys still prefer the old-fashioned type of girl. Who do you think is right?

Confused

Dear Confused:

_____

_____

_____

_____

_____

_____

_____

_____

The Adviser

B. Exchange your paragraph with a partner. Tell each other if you are convinced by the other person's opinions. Give each other advice on how to make your opinions stronger. Rewrite your response letters before you give them to your teacher.

You Be the Editor

Read the following letter. It contains eight mistakes. Find the mistakes and correct them. Then rewrite the corrected letter.

Dear Editor:

In my opinion, it is important for women with small childrens to work outside of the home. First of all, is to difficult to be with little kids all day. Womens needs a break from there kids. Also, a woman who has a career can offer her children mores. It is the quality of time that mothers spend with their children that are important.

Sincerely,

Lisa Harris

On Your Own

Write a paragraph giving your opinion on one of the following topics.

- marrying someone of a different religion
- eating a vegetarian diet
- what society should do about crime
- allowing women to serve in the military

CHAPTER 11

Comparing
and Contrasting

Similarities and Differences

Very often in your writing you will need to show how things are similar or different. When you *compare* two things, you show how they are similar. When you *contrast* two things, you show how they are different.

A. Study these two pictures. Look for similarities and differences.

COMPARING AND CONTRASTING **93**

B. Make a list of the similarities and another list of differences.

Similarities	Differences
_____	_____
_____	_____
_____	_____
_____	_____

Comparing

RECOGNIZING SIMILARITIES

A. Read the model paragraph.

Ann and Beth are identical twins, so it's easy to understand the embarrassing mistake I made yesterday. I was planning to ask Ann for a date, but it turned out I asked Beth. The two sisters look exactly alike. Both girls are tall and thin with short curly brown hair. They also have the same unusual blue-green eye color. In addition, Ann wears gold-rimmed glasses and so does Beth. Finally, both Ann and Beth have freckles. I wouldn't be surprised if they even have the exact same number of freckles. Now I have to explain my mistake to both of them.

B. What characteristics about Ann and Beth does the paragraph compare?

_____   _____

_____   _____

_____   _____

THE LANGUAGE OF COMPARISON

English uses special sentence patterns to make comparisons.

A. Study the following patterns of comparison using *and*.

<u>Affirmative sentences</u> *with the verb* **be**

Ann is a student. Beth is a student.

a. Ann is a student <u>and</u> Beth *is* <u>too</u>.

b. Ann is a student <u>and</u> <u>so</u> *is* Beth.

<u>Affirmative sentences</u> *with other verbs*

Japan exports cars. Germany exports cars.

a. Japan exports cars and Germany *does* <u>too</u>.

b. Japan exports cars <u>and</u> <u>so</u> *does* Germany.

<u>Negative sentences</u> *with the verb* **be**

The blue dress isn't expensive. The green dress isn't expensive.

a. The blue dress isn't expensive, <u>and</u> the green dress *isn't*, <u>either</u>.

b. The blue dress isn't expensive, <u>and neither</u> *is* the green dress.

<u>Negative sentences</u> *with other verbs*

Owls don't sleep at night. Mice don't sleep at night.

a. Owls don't sleep at night, <u>and</u> mice *don't* <u>either</u>.

b. Owls don't sleep at night, <u>and neither</u> *do* mice.

Practice using these structures. Follow the example.

Example

Ann runs four miles a day. Beth runs four miles a day.

a. <u>Ann runs four miles a day and Beth does too.</u>

b. <u>Ann runs four miles a day and so does Beth.</u>

1. Mark plays the piano. Dave plays the piano.

    a. _____

    b. _____

2. The bank opens at 9 A.M. The grocery store opens at 9 A.M.

    a. _____

    b. _____

3. Jamaica is sunny and beautiful. Hawaii is sunny and beautiful.

    a. _____

    b. _____

4. Peter doesn't smoke. Alex doesn't smoke.

    a. _____

    b. _____

5. Skiing is an exciting sport. Surfing is an exciting sport.

    a. _____

    b. _____

6. The Browns don't have a car. The Johnsons don't have a car.

    a. _____

    b. _____

7. Tunis is an old city. Cairo is an old city.

    a. _____

    b. _____

8. Suzanne lives in a small apartment. Amanda lives in a small apartment.

    a. _____

    b. _____

9. Charlie isn't friendly. Liz isn't friendly.

    a. _____

    b. _____

10. Children need love. Adults need love.

    a. _____

    b. _____

B. **Now study these patterns of comparison.**

the *same* + noun + *as*

Carla speaks the same <u>language</u> as José.
                         (noun)

This book is the same <u>price</u> as that one.

My house is the same <u>color</u> as yours.

as* + adjective/adverb + *as

Sam is as <u>tall</u> as his father.
          (adjective)

Pam is as <u>serious</u> as Anne.

Women's clothes are as <u>expensive</u> as men's clothes.

Dick drives as <u>carefully</u> as Mary.
                (adverb)

Charlotte dresses as <u>well</u> as Stephanie.

Practice using these patterns. Follow the example.

Example

Danny weighs 185 lbs. Arthur weighs 185 lbs.

   a. (noun: *weight*)   Danny is the same weight as Arthur.

   b. (adjective: *heavy*)   Danny is as heavy as Arthur.

1. Mary is five feet tall. John is five feet tall.

   a. (noun: *height*) _____

   b. (adjective: *tall*) _____

2. This car costs $8,500. That car costs $8,500.

   a. (noun: *price*) _____

   b. (adjective: *expensive*) _____

3. My house has eight rooms. Your house has eight rooms.

   a. (noun: *size*) _____

   b. (adjective: *big*) _____

4 Jeffrey was born in 1982. Paul was born in 1982.

   a. (noun: *age*) _____

   b. (adjective: *old*) _____

5. This story is seventy pages long. That story is seventy pages long.

   a. (noun: *length*) _____

   b. (adjective: *long*) _____

6. The teacher speaks loudly. The student speaks loudly.

   a. (noun: *voice*) _____

   b. (adverb: *loudly*) _____

SIGNAL WORDS OF COMPARISON

English uses many other special words and phrases to show comparison.

A. Study the following list:

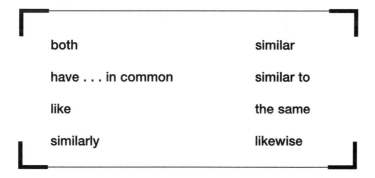

both	similar
have . . . in common	similar to
like	the same
similarly	likewise

B. Read the following model paragraph and underline all the expressions of comparison.

> The Reporter and The Monitor are very similar weekly magazines. First of all, they have many sections in common. For example, both magazines have sections on politics, finance, science, and culture. In addition, both of these popular magazines cost $4.99, and both are read by millions of people around the world. They also have the same cover story almost every week, and they usually review the same books and movies in their culture sections. Another similarity between the two magazines is their point of view. The Reporter is very conservative and so is The Monitor. Finally, both magazines are translated into ten languages.

C. Make a list of the similarities between the two magazines.

_____   _____

_____   _____

_____   _____

WRITING COMPARATIVE SENTENCES

A. These sentences are based on the paragraph above. Combine the sentences using the words in parentheses. You may need to refer back to the paragraph.

Example

> The Monitor and The Reporter are both weekly magazines. (and so)
> <u>The Monitor is a weekly magazine and so is The Reporter.</u>

1. Both The Monitor and The Reporter are weekly magazines. (and so)

_____

2. The Monitor and The Reporter report on political, financial, and cultural events of the world. (and . . . too)

_____

3. Both magazines cost $4.99. (the same . . . as)

_____

4. *The Reporter* is very conservative and so is *The Monitor*. (both)

_____

5. Both magazines are translated into ten languages. (as . . . as)

_____

B. Write a sentence of comparison for each of the following pairs of words. Use a variety of structures and vocabulary.

Example

The Empire State Building / the Statue of Liberty

The Empire State Building is in New York City and so is the Statue of Liberty.

1. England / United States

_____

2. Abraham Lincoln / John F. Kennedy

_____

3. lemons / bananas

_____

4. tennis / ping pong

_____

5. chemistry / biology

_____

C. Write four sentences comparing Jane Wexler and Ruth Friedman. Base your comparisons on the information provided on their driver's licenses.

ALABAMA STATE
Department of Motor Vehicles
DRIVER'S LICENSE

Eye color: **Brown**
Hair color: **Black**
Height: **5'3"**
Date of Birth: **6/30/61**

Jane Wexler

ALABAMA STATE
Department of Motor Vehicles
DRIVER'S LICENSE

Eye color: **Brown**
Hair color: **Black**
Height: **5'3"**
Date of Birth: **6/30/61**

Ruth Friedman

1. _____

2. _____

3. _____

4. _____

D. Study the following ads. Write four sentences of comparison based on your observations and the information provided.

1. _____

2. _____

3. _____

4. _____

WRITING TOPIC SENTENCES FOR COMPARISON PARAGRAPHS

When you write the topic sentence for a comparison paragraph, you must state the two things that you are comparing.

A. Look at the following sample topic sentences.

Time and *Newsweek* are very similar weekly magazines.
Time and *Newsweek* have several things in common.
Time and *Newsweek* are alike in many ways.
Time and *Newsweek* share many similarities.
Time is similar to *Newsweek* in several ways.

B. Write three different topic sentences for each of the following paragraphs.

1. _____. First of all, both cities are hot and humid most of the year. The typical daytime temperature in both places is about 92 degrees Fahrenheit (33 degrees Celsius) with humidity of 99 percent. It also rains a lot during the summer in Short Hills and White Plains. The evenings and nights are warm in both places.

   a. _____

   b. _____

   c. _____

2. _____. The main similarity is that both dogs are very friendly. Spot loves people, and so does Freckles. In addition, both of my dogs are smart and can do lots of tricks. For example, both can roll over on command. Another similarity is that both dogs are picky eaters. They only like the most expensive dog food.

a. _____

b. _____

c. _____

WRITING A PARAGRAPH OF COMPARISON

Prewriting

A. Study this biographical information about two important Americans, Benjamin Franklin and Thomas Jefferson.

BENJAMIN FRANKLIN

1706-1790

- founded University of Pennsylvania
- helped write Declaration of Independence
- important person in American Revolution
- well-known philosopher and thinker
- ambassador to France

THOMAS JEFFERSON

1743-1826

- author of Declaration of Independence
- third President of United States
- foreign Minister to France
- founded University of Virginia
- philosopher, architect, inventor
- played important role in American Revolution

B. Make a list of the similarities between the two men.

_____   _____

_____   _____

_____   _____

Writing

C. Complete the paragraph comparing these two famous Americans. Use your list of similarities as a guide.

Benjamin Franklin and Thomas Jefferson have many things in common. _____

_____

_____

_____

_____

_____

_____

_____

Revising

D. Read over your paragraph and look for ways to improve it. Use the revising checklist on page 44 to help you. Revise your paragraph and then rewrite it.

INDIVIDUAL ACTIVITY

Prewriting

A. Choose one of the following topics to compare.

- two similar movies you have seen
- two similar restaurants you have been to
- two similar teachers you have had
- two similar sports you enjoy
- two similar people you know

B. Before you begin to write the first draft of your paragraph, make a list of similarities between the two things you are comparing. (Look back at the lists of words to describe people, things, and places in Chapter 9.)

_____   _____

_____   _____

_____   _____

Writing

C. Now write a paragraph of comparison. Be sure to identify the two things you are comparing in the topic sentence. Then use the list of similarities from B as your guide.

READY
TO WRITE

_____

_____

_____

_____

_____

_____

Revising

D. Read over your paragraph and look for ways to improve it. Use the revising checklist on page 44 to help you. Revise your paragraph and then rewrite it.

Contrasting

When you describe the differences between two people, places, or things, you are contrasting them.

RECOGNIZING DIFFERENCES

A. Read the following model paragraph.

> When Michael was in Sedona last week, he ate at two very different restaurants. He had lunch at Cantina Italiana and dinner at the Cityside Café. First of all, the food at Cantina was delicious, but unfortunately, the food at Cityside was terrible. The atmosphere at Cantina Italiana was much better than the one at Cityside. Cantina was clean and quiet, however, the Cityside Café was dirty and noisy. The server at the Cantina Italiana was much more polite than the server at Cityside. In fact the server at Cityside was quite rude. Finally, the meal at Cityside Café was much more expensive than the meal at Cantina. Michael will always remember his delicious lunch at Cantina Italiana, but he can't wait to forget his terrible dinner at Cityside Café.

B. Make a list of the differences between the two restaurants.

Cantina Italiana	Cityside Café
_____	_____
_____	_____
_____	_____
_____	_____

THE LANGUAGE OF CONTRAST

Adjectives that are used to describe the differences between two people or things are called comparative adjectives.

A. Read the model paragraph.

> Sue and Linda are sisters, but they are different in many ways. For one thing, their physical appearances are very different. Sue is taller and thinner than Linda. Linda has darker eyes and longer hair than Sue. Their personalities are also different. Sue is more serious and more ambitious than Linda. She is a better student because she studies harder than her sister. On the other hand, Linda is more creative and more social than Sue.

To form comparative adjectives, follow these rules:

Add *–er* to one-syllable adjectives

hard → harder

Add *–ier* to adjectives that end in *y*

busy → busier

Add *more* in front of longer adjectives.

beautiful → more beautiful

Note these common exceptions:

Adjectives		Comparative Adjectives
good	→	better
well	→	better
bad	→	worse
far	→	farther, further

B. Reread the model paragraph and underline the comparative adjectives.

C. Practice using comparative patterns. Follow the example.

Example:

Gary weighs 178 lbs. Gerald weighs 165 lbs.

Gary is heavier than Gerald.

1. The Nile is 4,145 miles (6,669 kilometers) long. The Amazon is 3,915 miles (6,299 kilometers) long.

2. Mt. Everest is 29,025 feet (8,847 meters) high. Mt. Fuji is 12,389 feet (3,776 meters) high.

3. The third chapter is very difficult. The fourth chapter isn't as difficult.

_____

4. Ann is a very careful driver. Paul isn't a very careful driver.

_____

SIGNAL WORDS OF CONTRAST

English uses many signal words to show contrast.

although	*Although* my mother is talkative, my father is quiet.
however	My mother is talkative. *However*, my father is quiet.
on the other hand	My mother is talkative. *On the other hand*, my father is quiet.
but	My mother is talkative, *but* my father is quiet.
yet	My mother is talkative, *yet* my father is quiet.
different from	My mother's personality is *different* from my father's personality.
unlike	*Unlike* my mother, my father is quiet.

Underline the signal words that show contrast in the paragraph below.

The Reporter and *Style Magazine* are very different weekly magazines. First of all, they have different sections. *The Reporter* has sections on politics, finance, science, and culture. On the other hand, *Style* has sections on fashion, home decorating, cooking, and gardening. In addition, *The Reporter* costs $3.50 per issue, but *Style* costs $5.00 per issue. Finally, *The Reporter* is translated into ten languages, but *Style* is only in English.

WRITING CONTRAST SENTENCES

Write a sentence of contrast for each of the following pairs of words.

Example   feather / rock

A feather is lighter than a rock.

1. Alaska / Florida

_____

2. airplane / train

_____

3. classical music / rock 'n' roll

    _____

4. Volkswagen / Rolls Royce

    _____

5. ice cream / rice

    _____

WRITING TOPIC SENTENCES FOR CONTRAST PARAGRAPHS

When you write the topic sentence for a contrast paragraph you must state the two things that you are contrasting.

A. Look at the following list of sample topic sentences.

The Reporter and *Style* are very different weekly magazines.
The Reporter and *Style* are different in many ways.
The Reporter and *Style* have many differences.
The Reporter and *Style* differ in several ways.

B. Write three different topic sentences for each of the following paragraphs.

1. _____. First of all, the temperature in Westland is usually hotter than it is in Eastfalls. In Westland it is often in the nineties, but in Eastfalls, the temperature rarely goes above eighty. Secondly, the humidity is much higher in Westland than it is in Eastfalls. It rains a lot in Westland; however, it is usually dry in Eastfalls. Overall, the weather in Eastfalls is more pleasant.

    a. _____

    b. _____

    c. _____

2. _____. For one thing, they are different in appearance. Fluffy is a small, curly-haired dog, but Shane is big and shaggy. Another difference is their personality. Fluffy is very friendly and loves people. On the other hand, Shane is shy and afraid of people. Finally, my two dogs differ in their intelligence. Unlike Shane, Fluffy is smart and can do lots of tricks.

    a. _____

    b. _____

    c. _____

WRITING PARAGRAPHS OF CONTRAST

An Apartment

Prewriting

A. You and your friend are looking for an apartment to share near campus. You saw these two descriptions of apartments in the newspaper. Read the descriptions.

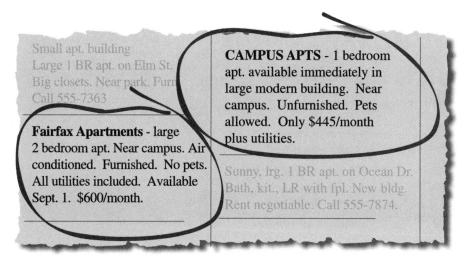

Small apt. building
Large 1 BR apt. on Elm St.
Big closets. Near park. Furn.
Call 555-7363

Fairfax Apartments - large 2 bedroom apt. Near campus. Air conditioned. Furnished. No pets. All utilities included. Available Sept. 1. $600/month.

CAMPUS APTS - 1 bedroom apt. available immediately in large modern building. Near campus. Unfurnished. Pets allowed. Only $445/month plus utilities.

Sunny, lrg. 1 BR apt. on Ocean Dr.
Bath, kit., LR with fpl. New bldg.
Rent negotiable. Call 555-7874.

B. Now write five sentences of contrast about the two apartments.

1. _____
2. _____
3. _____
4. _____
5. _____

Writing

C. Which apartment would you choose? Write a paragraph explaining your decision and the differences between the two apartments.

READY TO WRITE

_____
_____
_____
_____
_____
_____

Revising

D. Read over your paragraph and look for ways to improve it. Use the revising checklist on page 44 to help you. Revise your paragraph and then rewrite it.

A Trip to Hawaii

Prewriting

A. You and a friend are planning a trip to Hawaii. You found these advertisements in the newspaper. Read the advertisements.

B. Make a list of differences between the two trips.

_____   _____

_____   _____

_____   _____

Writing

C. Write a one-paragraph e-mail message to your friend contrasting the two plans and suggesting the one you think would be better for you.

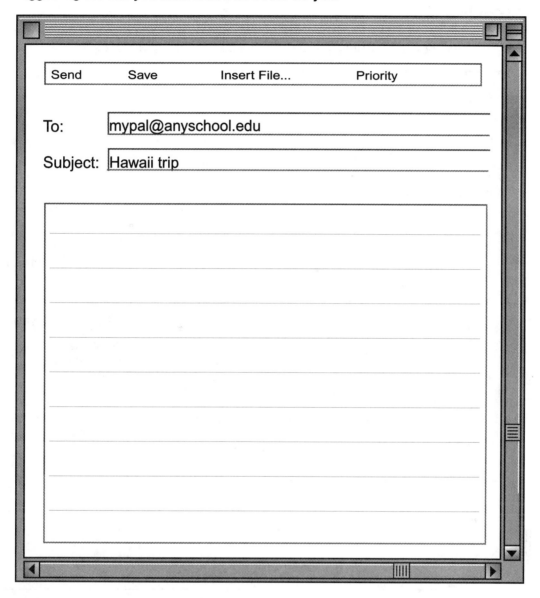

Send   Save   Insert File...   Priority

To: mypal@anyschool.edu

Subject: Hawaii trip

Revising

D. Read over your paragraph and look for ways to improve it. Use the revising checklist on page 44 to help you. Revise your paragraph and then rewrite it.

COMPARING ACTIVITY

Résumés

Prewriting

A. You are hiring a new English instructor for your school. You received the following two résumés from people applying for the job. Study the résumés.

Lynn Whitnall
Plaza de la Paz, No.2
CP 36000 Guanajuato
Gto, Mexico
Home Phone +52 (473) 732-02-13

POSITION DESIRED:
English Instructor

EDUCATION
1990 BA Spanish, New York University

EMPLOYMENT
1995–present, Spanish teacher, International High School

1992–1995   English Instructor, Tokyo Girls High School

1990–1992   Peace Corps volunteer in Colombia

OTHER
Fluent in Spanish, French, Japanese

AWARDS
Excellence in Teaching Award, 1999

Deborah Fines
42 St. James Place
Philadelphia, PA 19106

Position Desired:
English Instructor

Education:
1988–92   BA English, McGill University
1993   MA English, University of Toronto
1995   PhD Linguistics, University of Pennsylvania

Employment Experience
2000–present   Consultant and author
1995–2000   Instructor, Intensive English Program, University of Vermont
1994–1995   Teaching Assistant, Linguistics Department, University of Pennsylvania
1993–1994   Swimming Teacher
1988–1993   Server, *Chez Robert*

Publication:
English Verb Tenses, Shortman Publishing Company, 2001

Personal:
Fluent in French; competitive swimmer

B. Write five sentences of contrast based on the information in the résumés.

Example

Deborah has more degrees than Lynn.

1. _____

2. _____

3. _____

4. _____

5. _____

Writing

C. Who would you hire for the job? Write a paragraph supporting your decision.

_____

_____

_____

_____

_____

Revising

D. Read over your paragraph and look for ways to improve it. Use the revising checklist on page 44 to help you. Revise your paragraph and then rewrite it.

Contrasting Cultures

Prewriting

A. Talk to a classmate from another country. Discuss the differences between eating habits (or climate, social customs, family life, education, political system, or economy) in your culture and your partner's culture. If everyone in the class is from the same country, discuss the differences between your family and your partner's family. Make a list of the differences.

_____   _____

_____   _____

_____   _____

Writing

B. Write a paragraph of contrast. Use your list as a guide. Start with the biggest differences.

_____

_____

_____

_____

_____

_____

Revising

C. Ask your partner for suggestions to improve your paragraph. You can also use the revising checklist on page 44 to help you. Revise your paragraph and then rewrite it.

You Be the Editor

1. The following e-mail message has nine mistakes. Find the mistakes and correct them. Then rewrite the corrected message.

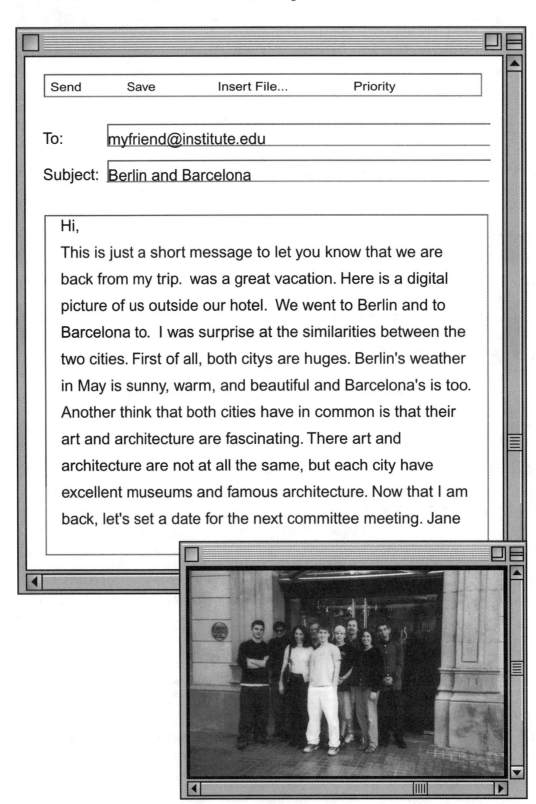

Send   Save   Insert File...   Priority

To: myfriend@institute.edu

Subject: Berlin and Barcelona

Hi,

This is just a short message to let you know that we are back from my trip. was a great vacation. Here is a digital picture of us outside our hotel. We went to Berlin and to Barcelona to. I was surprise at the similarities between the two cities. First of all, both citys are huges. Berlin's weather in May is sunny, warm, and beautiful and Barcelona's is too. Another think that both cities have in common is that their art and architecture are fascinating. There art and architecture are not at all the same, but each city have excellent museums and famous architecture. Now that I am back, let's set a date for the next committee meeting. Jane

2. **Read the following paragraph. It contains nine mistakes. Find the mistakes and correct them. Then rewrite the corrected paragraph.**

Francisco received a scholarship to study English in the United States. He had a difficulty time deciding whether he should attend the English program at Miami Community College in Miami, Florida or Rocky Mountain College in Denver, Colorado. It would be a lot cheapest for him to go to the community college, but he realize that his living expenses would be a lot more high in the city. Both schools has an excellent reputation, but Rocky Mountain is a much smaller school with a best student/teacher ratio. If he goes to the community college, he will not be as far away from home and he could go home more oftener. He also thought about how he would spend his free time. He might be happier, comfortabler, and more relaxed in the mountains. Finally, decided to attend Miami Community because the temperature is warmer in Florida and he is used to warm weather and water sports.

On Your Own

Choose one of the following topics to write about. You may write about either the similarities or the differences.

- two cities you have visited
- two vacations you have taken
- two jobs you have had
- two athletic teams you like
- two types of music

CHAPTER 12

Writing About Causes and Effects

Sometimes you will need to explain a situation by analyzing its causes (reasons) and its effects (results). To write a good explanation, you have to include the cause for a situation, as well as the effect.

Analyzing a Situation for Cause and Effect

Look at the two pictures below. The first picture shows a cause. The second picture shows an effect. State the cause and effect for each pair of pictures that follow.

Example

Cause: _The man found $100._   Effect: _The man is happy._

1. Cause: _____   Effect: _____

     _____   _____

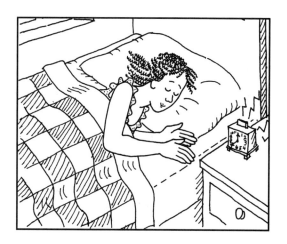

2. Cause: _____   Effect: _____

_____   _____

3. Cause: _____   Effect: _____

_____   _____

4. Cause: _____   Effect: _____

_____   _____

Analyzing Causes

Read the model paragraph and answer the questions.

> English is a difficult language to learn for several reasons. One reason is that the English spelling system is very irregular. Many English words sound the same but are spelled differently. For example, *hear* and *here* sound exactly the same, but they are spelled differently. In addition, English is difficult to learn because it has so many idioms. There are over 8,000 idioms in common use by English speakers. Last, and most importantly, English grammar is hard because it has many exceptions. For example, many English verbs are irregular. For every rule it seems that there are two exceptions. If learners know about these difficulties with English, they might feel less frustrated.

1. What is the topic sentence?

   _____

2. What causes (reasons) does the author give?

   _____

   _____

   _____

3. How are the causes organized?

   _____

SIGNAL WORDS THAT INTRODUCE A CAUSE

Study the following signal words and example sentences.

because	since	due to

Examples

I took my umbrella because it was raining.
Because it was raining, I took my umbrella.

I took my umbrella since it was raining.
Since it was raining, I took my umbrella.

I took my umbrella due to the rain.
Due to the rain, I took my umbrella.

I took my umbrella because of the rain.
Because of the rain, I took my umbrella.

WRITING SENTENCES OF CAUSE

Write a sentence of cause using *because* or *since* for each of the sets of pictures on pages 114 and 115.

Example

The man is happy because he found $100.

1. _____

2. _____

3. _____

4. _____

WRITING TOPIC SENTENCES FOR PARAGRAPHS ABOUT CAUSES

Here are some examples of topic sentences for paragraphs about causes.

- I decided to move to New York for several reasons.
- The economy is doing well for three main reasons.
- There are several causes of diabetes in adults.

Write a topic sentence for the following paragraphs.

1. _____

_____

Some people move because they want to find better jobs or to advance their careers. Others are attracted to new places because the weather is better. Still others want to move to a place with less crime. Finally, people often want to move to a place with a lower cost of living. For these reasons, every year millions of people pack up and move to new places.

2. _____

_____

One reason so many American children are overweight is that they eat too much junk food that is high in calories, sugar, and fat. Another reason is that many children do not get enough exercise. Because they spend so much time sitting in front of the television set or playing computer games, they do not move around very much. Genetics is another reason that children become overweight. Children whose parents or brothers or sisters are overweight may be at an increased risk of becoming overweight themselves.

WRITING A PARAGRAPH OF CAUSES

Your teacher will put this topic sentence on the board:

The world seems to be getting smaller for several reasons.

Prewriting

A. Think about the topic sentence. As a class, brainstorm reasons to support the topic sentence. Your teacher will write them in list form on the board. (Remember, these are just ideas, so they don't have to be in sentence form or correct order.) Copy the list here.

_____   _____

_____   _____

_____   _____

B. After you have a complete list of causes, discuss them. Decide which ones should be included in the paragraph. Cross out the ones that are not relevant.

Writing

C. Write a paragraph explaining the reasons the world seems smaller. Use your list as a guide. End with what you feel is the most important reason.

_____

_____

_____

_____

_____

_____

_____

_____

Revising

D. Read over your paragraph and look for ways to improve it. Use the revising checklist on page 44 to help you. Revise your paragraph and then rewrite it.

INDIVIDUAL ACTIVITY

In this activity you will analyze an important decision that you have made in your life.

Prewriting

A. Choose one of the following topics and make a list of reasons.

- reasons I got married
- reasons I came to this school
- reasons I chose this job
- reasons I chose my apartment or bought my house

Decision: _____

Reasons: _____   _____

        _____   _____

        _____   _____

        _____   _____

Writing

B. Write a first draft of your paragraph, using your list as a guide. Remember to begin with a topic sentence.

READY TO WRITE

_____

_____

_____

_____

_____

_____

_____

Revising

C. Give your paragraph to one of your classmates to read. Ask him or her to make suggestions about ways to improve the paragraph. You can also use the revising checklist on page 44 to help you. Revise your paragraph and then rewrite it.

SMALL GROUP ACTIVITY

You are a business administration student. You have been asked to analyze the following case history with a group of students.

Prewriting

A. Read the case.

CASE HISTORY #6

On September 5, Michael Williams opened a small compact disc shop in the basement of the Fairfax Apartment Building. The apartment building is located on a small side street just outside of town. It is three miles away from a large shopping center that has two discount compact disc stores.

Mr. Williams spent $10,000 buying CDs for his shop. Most of the CDs were rock 'n roll. He sold each CD for $8.00. He hired three people to work as salespersons and paid them $5.50 an hour. The shop was open Monday to Friday from 1 to 5 P.M. Mr. Williams would not accept checks or credit cards.

On December 19, Mr. Williams closed his shop. He put a sign on the door that said "Out of Business."

B. Discuss this case in your group. Why do you think the business failed? Make a list of the causes.

_____

_____

_____

_____

_____

_____

_____

_____

C. Now study this table and answer the questions.

Residents of the Fairfax by Age Groups

Age of Residents	Number of Residents
0–10	14
11–20	3
21–30	20
31–40	25
41–50	45
51–60	57
61 +	43

1. How can you describe the people who live in the Fairfax? What generalization can you make about the people?

_____

_____

_____

2. Can you use the information in this table to think of another cause of the failure of this business? Add it to your original list of causes.

_____

_____

_____

D. Now study this table.

Number of People Who Walk Past the Store							
	MON	TUES	WED	THURS	FRI	SAT	SUN
In the morning 8AM–12PM	30	35	28	29	31	32	20
In the afternoon 12PM–6PM	10	12	16	15	20	70	65
In the evening 6PM–12AM	40	47	53	42	60	65	40

E. Write three statements based on this table.

1. _____

2. _____

3. _____

Does the information in this table show another cause of the failure? What is it?

4. _____

Writing

READY TO WRITE

F. Write a first draft of a paragraph discussing the causes of the failure of Mr. Williams's compact disc shop.

_____

_____

_____

_____

_____

_____

_____

_____

Revising

G. Read over your group's paragraph and look for ways to improve it. Use the revising checklist on page 44 to help you. Revise the paragraph and then rewrite it.

Analyzing Effects

Read the model paragraph and answer the questions.

> Watching television can have several positive effects on students learning English. One effect is that students can improve their pronunciation by listening to the people on television. In addition, students can observe gestures and body language that are part of communication. Most importantly, students are exposed to a wide variety of idioms that are commonly used by English speakers.

1. What is the topic sentence?

_____

2. What effects does the author give?

_____ _____

_____ _____

_____ _____

3. What kind of order does the author use to explain the effects.

_____

SIGNAL WORDS THAT INTRODUCE AN EFFECT

so	therefore	as a result
thus	consequently	

Examples

Mrs. Baker has an ulcer, *so* she avoids spicy food.

Mrs. Baker has an ulcer. *Therefore,* she avoids spicy food.
                       Thus,
                       Consequently,
                       As a result,

Mrs. Baker has an ulcer; *therefore,* she avoids spicy food.
                       thus,
                       consequently,
                       as a result,

WRITING SENTENCES OF CAUSE AND EFFECT

A.   Look at this cartoon. Complete the sentences that follow with *so* or *therefore*.

1. There are no ice cubes in Snoopy's water, _____ he is angry.

2. There are no ice cubes in Snoopy's water; _____, he is angry.

3. There are no ice cubes in Snoopy's water. _____, he is angry.

B. Write a sentence of cause and effect using *so* or *therefore* for each of the sets of pictures on pages 114 and 115.

Example

The man found $100; therefore, he is happy.

1. _____

2. _____

3. _____

4. _____

C. Match the causes and effects. The first one has been done for you.

Effects	Causes
1. ___d___ I'm going skiing today.	a. It was faster than the train.
2. _____ We moved to the country.	b. He likes to get exercise in the morning.
3. _____ We bought a new car.	c. The city was too crowded.
4. _____ They took an airplane.	d. It snowed five inches last night.
5. _____ She doesn't eat desserts.	e. It didn't rain enough this summer.
6. _____ The flowers in our garden died.	f. The old one used too much gas.
7. _____ He took an aspirin.	g. She's on a diet.
8. _____ He rides his bike to work.	h. He has a toothache.
9. _____ It is very hot today.	i. We turned on the air conditioner.

Now combine the causes and effects to make new sentences. Use *so*, *because*, or *therefore*.

1. It snowed five inches last night, so I'm going skiing today.

2. _____

3. _____

4. _____

5. _____

6. _____

7. _____

8. _____

9. _____

WRITING TOPIC SENTENCES FOR PARAGRAPHS ABOUT EFFECTS

Here are some examples of topic sentences for paragraphs about effects.

- Computers have had several important effects on society.
- There are a number of consequences of global warming.
- The birth of my twins has had several effects on my life.
- The flood caused several problems in our town.

Write a topic sentence for the following paragraphs.

1. _____.

   For one thing, there was so much snow that it was dangerous to drive and several main roads had to be closed. In addition, students had the day off because all the schools were closed. Finally, the snowstorm cost the city a lot of money to clean up.

2. _____.

   First of all, running increases the efficiency of the heart and lungs. Running also helps the body develop greater physical endurance. Finally, it helps the body become more mechanically efficient.

3. _____.

   I have to be at work earlier in the morning, and I have much more responsibility. It also means that I make more money. All things considered, this is a great opportunity and I am very happy with my new job.

RECOGNIZING IRRELEVANT SENTENCES

The following paragraphs each contain one sentence that is irrelevant. Cross out that sentence and be prepared to explain why it does not belong in the paragraph.

1.   There are several reasons why many American women are waiting until they are thirty years old or older to have their first baby. Some women have good jobs and want to continue their careers. Many American couples have two children. Other women don't want the responsibility of having children until they are older. Still others are waiting until they are financially secure before they start a family. Increased personal and professional opportunities for women often result in delaying motherhood.

2.   Listening to music can have many positive effects on children. For one thing, listening to music can increase verbal, emotional, and spatial intelligence. Some children prefer sports to music. It can also improve concentration and stimulate creative thinking. Finally, another positive effect of music is that it can relax children and make them feel more comfortable. Some scientists think music can even improve children's memory. Overall, it seems music is beneficial to children's learning and sense of well-being.

3.   The introduction of affordable automobiles had several effects on North American society. First of all, automobiles created a more mobile society. Automobiles made it possible for people to move out of the cities and into the suburbs. Automobiles also affected the growth of new businesses. Gas stations, auto repair shops, and roadside restaurants became necessary. Railroads had a great effect on society too. In addition, new roads were built as a result of the increase in the number of cars. All of these changes meant that the automobile was transforming the lifestyle of millions of North Americans.

WRITING EFFECTS PARAGRAPHS

Prewriting

A.   Your teacher will put this topic sentence on the board:

There are several effects of pollution.

B.   What effects can you and your classmates think of? Brainstorm a list of effects. Your teacher will write them in list form on the board. (Remember, these are just ideas, so they don't have to be in sentence form or correct order.) Copy the list here.

_____   _____

_____   _____

_____   _____

C.   After you have a complete list of effects, discuss them. Decide which should be included in the paragraph. Cross out the ones that are not strong or relevant.

Writing

D.   Write a paragraph about the effects of pollution, using your list as a guide. End with what you feel is the most important effect.

_____

_____

_____

_____

_____

_____

_____

_____

Revising

E. Read over your paragraph and look for ways to improve it. Use the revising checklist on page 44 to help you. Revise your paragraph and then rewrite it.

ANALYZING EFFECTS

The Effects of Sugar

Prewriting

A. Read the following list of facts about white sugar.

- robs the body of vitamin B
- causes tooth decay
- interferes with calcium metabolism
- contributes to hardening of arteries

B. Use the list to write a paragraph about the effects of white sugar on the human body. Begin with a topic sentence.

_____

_____

_____

_____

_____

_____

_____

_____

Revising

C. Read over your paragraph and look for ways to improve it. Use the revising checklist on page 44 to help you. Revise your paragraph and then rewrite it.

The Effects of a Decision

Prewriting

A. Choose one of the following topics and make a list of the effects that decision has had on your life.

- getting married
- choosing a career
- buying a house
- picking a school
- coming to an English-speaking country

_____   _____

_____   _____

_____   _____

Writing

B. Write a first draft of your paragraph, using your list as a guide. Remember to begin with a topic sentence.

_____

_____

_____

_____

_____

_____

_____

Revising

C. Give your paragraph to one of your classmates to read. Ask him or her to make suggestions about ways to improve the paragraph. You can use the revising checklist on page 44 to help you. Revise your paragraph and then rewrite it.

SMALL GROUP ACTIVITY

Prewriting

A. Read the following information.

> Acton is a small town in the Midwest. It has a population of 2,500. It is a safe, quiet, and clean place to live. Most of the people have lived there all their lives and know each other very well. The town has not changed very much in the past one hundred years.
>
> Last month, Stanley Manufacturing decided to open a large factory in Acton. This will bring many new people to the community. Some people are worried about the negative effects the new factory will have on the town. Other people are excited about the positive effects the new factory will have on Acton.

B. In small groups make predictions about the impact the new factory will have on Acton. Make a list of all the possible effects you can think of.

Positive	Negative
more jobs	pollution

Writing

C. Choose one of the groups below.

1. You are a group of conservative residents who doesn't want Acton to change. On a separate piece of paper, write a paragraph predicting the negative effects the factory will have on the town.

2. You are a group of progressive residents who is open to changes in your community. On a separate piece of paper, write a paragraph predicting the positive effects the new factory will have on the town.

Revising

D. Read over your group's paragraph and look for ways to improve it. Use the revising checklist on page 44 to help you. Revise your paragraph and then rewrite it.

PAIR ACTIVITY

Prewriting

A. Look at the diagram below. It shows how plants and animals depend on each other in a farm pond. Discuss the diagram with a classmate. Imagine that you have been asked to write a short explanation of this diagram for a children's science magazine.

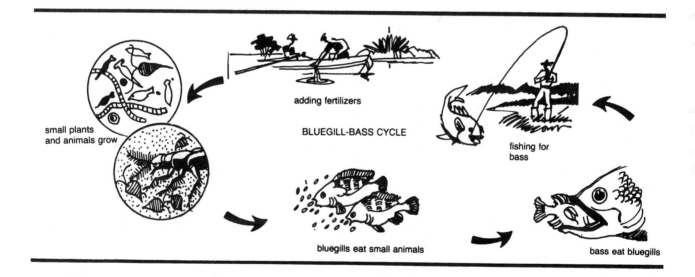

small plants
and animals grow

adding fertilizers

BLUEGILL-BASS CYCLE

fishing for
bass

bluegills eat small animals

bass eat bluegills

B. Make a list of the effects that plants and animals in the pond have on each other.

_____   _____

_____   _____

_____   _____

Writing

C. Write a paragraph about the ecological relationships that are shown in the diagram on page 129. Begin with a topic sentence.

_____

_____

_____

_____

_____

_____

_____

Revising

D. Read over your paragraph with your partner and look for ways to improve it. Use the revising checklist on page 44 to help you. Revise your paragraph and then rewrite it.

JUST FOR FUN

Match the questions in column A with the answers in column B.

A		B
1 ____	Why did the man cross the street?	a. His head is so far from his body.
2. ____	Why did the man throw the clock out the window?	b. They live in schools.
3. ____	Why does the giraffe have such a long neck?	c. He wanted to see time fly.
4. ____	Why did the man tiptoe past the medicine cabinet?	d. He wanted to get to the other side.
5. ____	Why are fish smarter than insects?	e. He didn't want to wake up the sleeping pills.
6. ____	Why is a library the tallest building?	f. It has the largest number of stories.

You Be the Editor

Read the following article. It contains seven mistakes. Find the mistakes and correct them. Then rewrite the corrected article.

DEADLY SURPRISE TORNADO

August 3. The tornado that hit kansas today surprised even the weather forecasters. The violent winds blowed over 200 miles per hour. Much crops were destroyed by the storm. Hundreds of people lost his homes or offices because of the high winds and heavy rains. The Red Cross estimates that the killer storm caused many injuries. Also, million of dollars worth of farm animals were killed due to the tornado. will take the people of Kansas many time to recover from the effects of this tornado.

On Your Own

Choose one of these topics and write a paragraph.

- causes or effects of immigrating to a new country
- causes or effects of bad health habit (smoking, overeating, drinking too much)
- causes or effects of a recent economic or political situation in your country or a country you know well.

CHAPTER 13

Writing Personal and Business Letters

In this chapter you will learn how to write two kinds of letters—personal letters and business letters.

Personal Letters

Personal letters are often called "friendly letters." They are letters that you write to a friend or relative. Personal letters include information about you, and ask questions about how your friend or relative is doing. Personal letters are informal and do not have to be typed. There are five main parts to a personal letter. The parts are labeled on the model letter below.

September 8, 2002] date

Dear Daniel,] greeting

   Thank you very much for the wonderful week I spent with you and your family. Your mother is such a terrific cook! I think I must have gained 10 pounds in just the seven days I spent with you. I really appreciate your taking time off from work to take me around and show me so many places. You are lucky to live in such an interesting area. I hope that soon you will be able to visit my part of the country. Thank you again for a wonderful time. Let's keep in touch.] message

Best regards,] closing

Matthew] signature

Remember these guidelines when you write a personal letter:

- The date goes in the upper right corner. (The month is capitalized, and a comma goes between the day and the year.)
- The greeting (Dear _____) is followed by a comma.
- The closing (often "Love" in personal letters) is followed by a comma.

Use the following form for the envelope of a personal letter:

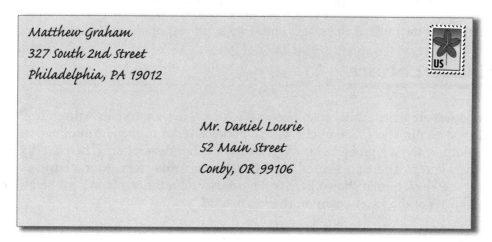

Matthew Graham
327 South 2nd Street
Philadelphia, PA 19012

Mr. Daniel Lourie
52 Main Street
Conby, OR 99106

Don't forget:

- The return address of the person who writes the letter goes in the upper left corner.
- The address of the person who will receive the letter goes in the center of the envelope.
- The stamp goes in the upper right corner.

WRITING A PERSONAL LETTER

Write a personal letter to a friend you haven't seen recently. Tell him or her what is new in your life. Also, ask some questions about his or her life.

READY TO WRITE

_____

_____

_____

_____

_____

_____

_____

_____

_____

_____

On Your Own

Write a short letter to each of the following people. Bring your finished letters to class in properly addressed envelopes.

- A friend. Invite him or her to come visit you.
- Your aunt. Thank her for the gift she sent you.
- Your parents. Tell them about an important decision you have made.

Exchange letters with a classmate and write short responses to the letters.

Business Letters

Business letters are more formal than personal letters. They are usually written to someone you do not know. You might write a business letter to request information or to inform someone about a problem. Look at the model business letter. There are six parts to a business letter. There are several acceptable formats you can use for a business letter, but the block format shown here is the easiest and most common. In the block format, all parts of the letter begin on the left margin.

177 Atlantic Avenue
Boston, Massachusetts 02140
April 22, 2002 } heading

Director of Admissions
Harvard University
Cambridge, Massachusetts 02138 } inside address

Dear Sir or Madam: } greeting

    I am a senior at Springfield Academy and I am interested in attending Harvard University to study business. Please send me the appropriate application forms and any information you have about the undergraduate business program. I will also need information about TOEFL requirements because English is not my native language. } message

I look forward to hearing from you.

Sincerely, } closing

Hasan Halkali

Hasan Halkali } signature

Remember these guidelines for writing business letters:

- Use a colon after the greeting.
- Identify yourself and state the purpose of your letter at the beginning. Go directly to the point. Be brief and clear.
- Type business letters if possible.
- Do not ask personal information (age, health, family) of the person you are writing to.
- Do not use slang, informal phrases, or contractions.

IDENTIFYING FORMAL AND INFORMAL PHRASES

In each pair of sentences or phrases below, one should be used only in informal letters. The other one is appropriate for formal letters. Put an *F* in front of the one that is formal and an *I* in front of the one that is informal.

1. _____ I'm really sorry about what happened.

   _____ I would like to apologize for the inconvenience this caused you.

2. _____ I look forward to hearing from you soon.

   _____ I can't wait to hear from you.

3. _____ Dear Julie,

   _____ Dear Mrs. Brody:

4. _____ Yours truly,

   _____ Love,

5. _____ I will call you Monday morning.

   _____ I'll give you a call next week.

6. _____ I appreciate your help in this matter.

   _____ Thanks a lot for helping me.

WRITING A BUSINESS LETTER

A. Read the advertisement for the Philadelphia Orchestra.

SEE THE

Philadelphia Orchestra
ACADEMY OF MUSIC

HURRY !
ORDER TICKETS NOW!

1420 Locust St.,
Phila., Pa 19102

EVENINGS—8 PM

MATINEES—
Wed, Sat,
and Sun 3 PM

PRICES	Orchestra & Mezzanine	Balcony
Evenings		
MON–THURS	$30	$25
FRI–SAT	$32	$27
Matinees		
WED	$25	$20
SAT	$27	$22
SUN	$30	$25

**READY
TO WRITE**

B. Write a letter requesting tickets. In your letter you will need to state the following:

- the date of the performance you want to attend
- whether you want a matinee or an evening performance
- which price ticket you want
- whether you are including your credit card number or a personal check

_____

_____

_____

_____

_____

_____

_____

_____

_____

_____

_____

_____

_____

_____

Revising

C. Read your letter again. Consider the following questions and make corrections if necessary.

- Have you included both a heading and an inside address? Are they in the proper places?
- Is there a colon after the greeting?
- Is your letter direct and to the point?
- Is the closing followed by a comma?
- Did you sign your letter?

D. Revise your letter and then rewrite it.

On Your Own

A. Write about one of the following situations.

- Write to a college admissions office asking for information.
- Write to a radio station requesting more information about a product you heard advertised.
- Write a letter to a magazine publisher stating that you ordered a magazine subscription three months ago but haven't received a magazine yet.
- Write a letter of importance to you.

B. When you have finished the letter, review the questions in part C above. Make corrections if necessary.

C. Bring your finished letter to class in a properly addressed envelope. (Use the same format for a business letter envelope that you use for a personal letter envelope.) Exchange letters with a classmate and give each other suggestions for making your letters clearer.

LETTERS OF COMPLAINT

A. Imagine yourself in the following situation:

Two weeks ago you called the person who lives above you in your apartment building. You were upset because he plays his stereo so loudly. He plays it very loudly all day long so it bothers you when you are trying to study. He also plays it late at night when you are trying to sleep. When you spoke with him on the phone, he said that he would try to keep the volume lower. The first few days it was better, but now it is becoming a problem again. Also, you are trying to study for your final exam. It is very difficult because of the constant noise.

B. Write a polite letter to him asking him to please be more considerate.

_____

_____

_____

_____

_____

_____

_____

_____

_____

C. It is now one week later and the noise has gotten even worse. You are furious. Write an angry letter to your landlord threatening to break your lease and move out if he or she does not do something about the noise. Since this is a business letter, don't forget the heading and the inside address. Remember to type the final copy of a business letter.

_____

_____

_____

_____

_____

_____

_____

_____

_____

_____

_____

_____

_____

_____

You Be the Editor

1. **Read the following personal letter. It contains seven mistakes. Correct the mistakes and rewrite the corrected letter.**

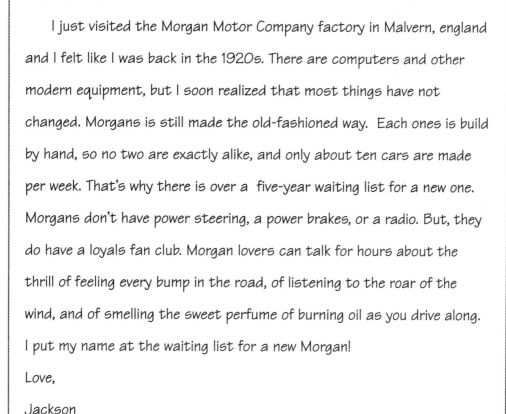

June 10, 2002

Dear Isabelle:

I just visited the Morgan Motor Company factory in Malvern, england and I felt like I was back in the 1920s. There are computers and other modern equipment, but I soon realized that most things have not changed. Morgans is still made the old-fashioned way. Each ones is build by hand, so no two are exactly alike, and only about ten cars are made per week. That's why there is over a five-year waiting list for a new one. Morgans don't have power steering, a power brakes, or a radio. But, they do have a loyals fan club. Morgan lovers can talk for hours about the thrill of feeling every bump in the road, of listening to the roar of the wind, and of smelling the sweet perfume of burning oil as you drive along. I put my name at the waiting list for a new Morgan!

Love,

Jackson

2. **Read the following business letter. It contains eight mistakes. Correct the mistakes and rewrite the corrected letter.**

1123 Gardner Street

Swansea, Massachusetts 02777

March 2, 2002

Youth Fair Cosmetics Company

234 Philip Place

New York, New York

Dear Sir or Madam,

I have been using youth fair products for many years and I have always been very pleased with them. However, last week I bought a bottle of your newest perfume, Rose Petal, and had terribly results. First, it stained my blouse. It also cause my skin to itch and burn. Worst of all, I couldn't stop sneezing after used it. I feel that this product does not meet your standards of high quality and I would appreciate receiving a refund. I look forward to hearing from you on this matter in the near future.

sincerely

Charlotte Sherden

Charlotte Sherden

CHAPTER 14

Writing Summaries

Summaries

Summaries require a special kind of writing. A good summary gives only main ideas. It does not include details. Before you begin to write a summary, you should think about *who, when, where, why, what,* and *how*.

DISTINGUISHING BETWEEN MAIN IDEAS AND DETAILS

A. Read the article below. As you read, underline only the main ideas.

Dog Hero is Honored

This dog hero was only 9 months old when he performed his brave act. Bo, a Labrador Retriever, won the annual hero award from the Ken-L Ration dog food company. His prizes included a gold medal, a gold collar and leash, and a year's supply of dog food! He also won $5000 for his owners.

Bo did his brave deed last June. Bo and his owners, Rob and Laurie Roberts, were going down the Colorado River rapids in a 16-foot boat. The Roberts family lives near the river in Glenwood Springs, Colorado. Both of the Roberts, and Bo, are good swimmers. The Roberts also love boating. The June trip was Bo's first time in a boat.

Things were fine until, as Laurie Roberts said, "A six-foot wave broke in front of us and filled the boat with water. Another big wave caught us from the back and flipped the boat over." Rob was thrown clear, but Laurie and Bo were trapped under it. "Every time I tried to escape, my head hit the boat," Laurie said. "I hit the bottom of the river several times. I realized I was drowning."

Rob picks up the story. "I reached the shore and looked for Laurie," he said. "I saw Bo swim out from under the overturned boat. Then he turned around and dived. Soon he came back up, pulling Laurie by

the hair." Laurie, scared and breathless, tried to grab Bo. But the dog stayed out of reach, as if knowing they would both drown if Laurie pulled him under. Finally Laurie grabbed Bo's tail. He dragged her 30 yards to shore. Laurie was cut and bleeding, but she wasn't badly hurt.

"If it hadn't been for Bo, I wouldn't be here," Laurie told the audience at the Dog Hero awards dinner.

Ken-L Ration has been giving Dog Hero awards for 29 years. In that time, hero dogs have been honored for saving the lives of 306 people.

B. Read the statements about the story on page 141. Put *MI* next to sentences that are main ideas. Put *D* next to sentences that give details.

_____ 1. Bo's prizes included a gold medal, a gold collar and leash, and a year's supply of dog food.

_____ 2. Bo won the annual hero award from the Ken-L Ration dog food company.

_____ 3. Rob and Laurie Roberts are good swimmers.

_____ 4. Bo saved Laurie's life when he rescued her from a boating accident.

_____ 5. Bo dragged Laurie 30 yards.

_____ 6. Ken-L Ration has given Dog Hero awards for 29 years.

_____ 7. Bo's brave deed happened last June.

_____ 8. Bo and his owners were going down the Colorado River rapids in a 16-foot boat.

_____ 9. Hero dogs have been honored for saving the lives of 306 people.

C. Complete the summary below.

Rob and Laurie Roberts's dog, _____, (who) won the annual Ken-L Ration _____ (what) for saving Laurie's life _____. (when) Roberts and Bo were on the _____ (where) when their boat was hit by a big wave. The boat turned over and Laurie was trapped underneath. Bo rescued Laurie and dragged her to _____. (where)

WRITING A SUMMARY

Prewriting

A. Read the following article from an ecology textbook.

WHY DO SOME ANIMALS DIE OUT?

It is natural for species of animals to become extinct over millions of years. But, in the past 200 years, humans have caused the process to speed up. In recent years, the total number of threatened animal species has increased from 5,205 to 5,435. Today 25 percent (one in four) of mammal species and 12 percent (one in eight) of bird species are threatened with extinction. In most cases this is a result of human activity. How are people accelerating the process of animal extinction?

First of all, people threaten the survival of animal species by destroying their habitats. As human populations grow, people keep building houses and factories in fields and woods. As they spread over the land, they destroy animals' homes. If the animals can't find a place to live, they die out. Sixteen kinds of Hawaiian birds have become extinct for this reason. Other animals, such as the Florida Key deer, may soon die out because they are losing their homes.

Overhunting is another way that humans are causing some animals to become extinct. In some parts of the world, the parts of rare animals are worth a lot of money. For example, some people will pay more than $1,000 for a single rhino horn. This encourages hunters to kill rhinos even though they face extinction. Other animals that are threatened with extinction from overhunting include the blue whale, the mountain gorilla, and the cheetah.

Humans are also polluting the air, water, and soil. The effect of pollution on animal species can be complicated. For example, when waste from factories is dumped into rivers, the rivers become polluted. The fish that live in the river are poisoned and many of them die. In addition, birds that eat the poisoned fish become poisoned themselves. Once they are poisoned, these birds cannot lay strong, healthy eggs. Fewer and fewer new birds are born. So far, no animals have become extinct because of pollution. But some, such as the brown pelican, have become rare and may die out.

Finally, when humans introduce new species into certain environments, the animals that already live there become threatened and face extinction. For example, when Europeans settlers brought rabbits and foxes to Australia, they killed off many native Australian animals, including the bandicoot. The rabbits and foxes adapted to the Australian environment very quickly and multiplied rapidly. Eventually, the foxes hunted and killed many bandicoots for food. The rabbits took over the bandicoot habitats. Now the bandicoots are threatened with extinction in their own land.

B. Now answer the following questions.

1. What is the article about?

   _____

2. Why is it happening?

   _____

3. Who is responsible?

   _____

4. When is it happening?

   _____

Writing

C. Write a one-paragraph summary of the article. State the main idea of the article in the first sentence. Answer the questions *what*, *when*, and *how* in the rest of the paragraph.

READY TO WRITE

_____

_____

_____

_____

_____

_____

_____

_____

_____

Revising

D. Did you answer all of the questions in Exercise B? Look at the revising checklist on page 44. Exchange papers with a partner and edit each other's papers. Did you both include the same information? If not, what were the differences? Revise your paragraph and then rewrite it.

SUMMARIZING THE NEWS

Prewriting

A. Read this short newspaper article.

HURRICANE STRIKES—MANY HURT

Hurricane Irene hit southeastern Florida on Friday night, causing damage and destruction everywhere. The storm dumped 18 inches of rain on the area. The high winds that blew up to 85 miles per hour were responsible for most of the damage to the area. The winds knocked down trees and power lines, broke hotel windows, and damaged roofs. The wind also was to blame for ten serious injuries and several car accidents.

Much of the city was without electricity and water this morning. In fact, hundreds of thousands of people have no electricity.

The hurricane caused severe flooding. Hundreds of people lost their homes or offices because of high winds and heavy rains. Some of the worst flooding was in Miami, where police sometimes needed boats to get through up to 4 feet of standing water.

Thousands of acres of crops were damaged or destroyed in South Florida, which supplies 75 percent of the nation's winter produce. No one knows yet exactly how much money was lost in crop damage. "I could not give you an estimate of damage to the crops, but I would not be surprised if it were $100 million," said the mayor of Miami.

Local officials called Irene the worst storm of the hurricane season for the area. It will take the people of Florida a long time to recover from the effects of this hurricane.

Prewriting

B. Make a list of the important facts in the article. Try to include *who, what, when, where, why,* and *how* on our list.

_____

_____

_____

_____

_____

C. Study your list. Make sure you have included only the main ideas. Cross out any items on your list that are details.

Writing

D. Write a short, one-paragraph summary of the article.

_____

_____

_____

_____

_____

Revising

E. Compare your summary with some of your classmates' summaries. Have you included too much information? Did you miss an important idea? Revise your summary paragraph and then rewrite it.

On Your Own

Find an article in a book, magazine, or newspaper. Read it carefully and write a one-paragraph summary of it. Bring the article and your summary to class. Exchange summaries with a classmate and give each other suggestions for improving the summary.

Answering Test Questions

Teachers and professors often ask you to answer questions in paragraph form on tests. There are several important things to remember when answering test questions.

- Read the entire question carefully.
- Make sure you understand exactly what information you are being asked to write about (reasons, definitions, etc.).
- Plan your answer.
- Budget your time.

BEGINNING THE ESSAY

You will find that the easiest way to begin your essay is to change the question to a statement and use this statement as your topic sentence. (Often the "question" is not written in question form, but in the imperative form.) Study the example.

Example

Question: Discuss why Americans move so often.

Topic sentence: There are many reasons why Americans move often.

Change the following essay questions into topic sentences.

1. Question: Discuss why many women are waiting until after they are thirty years old to have children.

Topic Sentence: _____

2. Question: Discuss the effects of radiation on the human body.

Topic Sentence: _____

3. Question: Explain the reasons ice hockey is a dangerous sport.

Topic Sentence: _____

4. Question: Explain the importance of John F. Kennedy in American history.

Topic Sentence: _____

5. Question: Discuss the reasons why so many tourists visit Brazil.

Topic Sentence: _____

6. Question: Explain the reasons for the popularity of video games.

Topic Sentence: _____

7. Question: Discuss the advantages and disadvantages of solar energy.

Topic Sentence: _____

8. Question: Describe the four kinds of clouds.

Topic Sentence: _____

9. Question: Describe the four stages involved in cell division.

Topic Sentence: _____

THE PARTS OF THE TEST ANSWER

Read the following test question and student response. Then answer the questions that follow.

Question:

Discuss the three stages of sending a spacecraft into orbit.

Student Answer:

There are three stages involved in sending a spacecraft into orbit. First, the Stage One Rocket is used for the blastoff, but it is only used for two and a half minutes. When the spacecraft reaches a speed of 6,000 miles per hour and an altitude of forty miles, this rocket drops off into the sea. Then, the Stage Two Rocket is used, but only for about six minutes, because it drops off when the spacecraft reaches a speed of 14,000 miles per hour and an altitude of 110 miles. Finally, during the third stage, the spacecraft goes into orbit. The Stage Three Rocket is used for two minutes, or until the spacecraft reaches a speed of 17,500 miles per hour and an altitude of 120 miles.

1. What is the topic sentence?

   _____

2. Does it restate the question?

   _____

3. Underline the signal words the student used.

   _____

4. What specific information (details such as numbers and times) did the student include?

   _____   _____

   _____   _____

   _____   _____

WRITING A RESPONSE TO A TEST QUESTION

Discuss the many similarities between the eye and the camera. Base your answer on the following information.

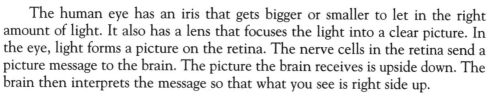

READY
TO WRITE

The eye

The human eye has an iris that gets bigger or smaller to let in the right amount of light. It also has a lens that focuses the light into a clear picture. In the eye, light forms a picture on the retina. The nerve cells in the retina send a picture message to the brain. The picture the brain receives is upside down. The brain then interprets the message so that what you see is right side up.

The camera

The camera has a diaphragm that gets bigger or smaller to let in the right amount of light. It also has a lens that focuses the light into a clear picture. In a camera, light forms a picture on film. The picture is upside down on the film.

_____

_____

_____

_____

_____

_____

_____

_____

_____

You Be the Editor

Read the following article about electronic mail. It contains ten mistakes. Find the mistakes and correct them. Then rewrite the article.

Experts say that the use of electronic mail (also known as "e-mail") is growing dramatically. According to the Yankee Group, a Boston market-research company, the number of E-mail users in U.S. raised by 60 percents from 5.9 millions to 9.4 millions between 1992 and 1993, and it increased other 60 percent in 1993. Billions of messages are now transmitted day in North America. That is three times the number of letters sent by regular mail. E-mail is become more and more valuable because it makes communication so much easyier.

Answer Key

CHAPTER 3, page 26—You Be the Editor

(T)hroughout history, people have found it necessary to do mathematical computations and keep accounts. (I)n early times, we used groups of sticks or stones to help make calculations. (T)hen the abacus was developed in (C)hina. (T)hese simple methods represent the beginnings of data processing. (A)s computational needs became more complicated, we developed more advanced technologies. (O)ne example is the first simple adding machine that (B)laise (P)ascal developed in (F)rance in 1642. (A)nother example is the first machine that would do calculations and print out results, which (C)harles (B)abbage designed in (E)ngland in 1830. (I)n the middle of the twentieth century, researchers at the (U)niversity of (P)ennsylvania built the first electronic computer. (T)oday, of course, we have the computer to perform all kinds of advanced mathematical computations.

CHAPTER 4, page 33—You Be the Editor

Erik enjoy~s~ many types of sports. He is ~~liking~~ likes team sport~s~ such as basketball, soccer, and baseball. He also plays traditional~s~ individual sports like raquetball and golf. ~~his~~ His favorite sports involve danger as well as ~~exciting~~ excitement. He loves extreme skiing, and skydiving.

CHAPTER 5, page 39—You Be the Editor

My office is small, but it is ~~comfortably~~ comfortable. There are two big~s~ windows on the left and one small window directly in front of you. ~~my~~ My desk fits perfectly under the two big windows. Since my computer is on my desk~x~, I can look out the window as I work. I have a small couch on the wall opposite the desk. Next to the couch, there ~~are~~ is a bookcase.

Do Diets Work?

Doctors and dieters agree that~it.~is possible to lose weight by dieting. The ~~difficulty~~ *difficult* part, they report, is keeping the weight ~~of~~ *off* after you ~~to~~ lose it.

Research indicates that many people successfully lose weight at some point in life, but most people gain the weight back within three years. Ian Fenn is a doctor who specializes in weight problems. He says that there ~~is~~ *are* many sorts of diets, and medical science is working to figure out how to control body weight. "It is also a matter," he says, "of getting people to change their lifestyles. Each person need*s* to find the right combination of diet and exercise."

It is not difficult to remove the shell from a lobster if you follow these step*s*. First, you should ~~to~~ put the lobster on ~~it's~~ *its* back and remove the two large claws and tail section. After that, ~~You~~ *you* must also twist off the flippers at *the* end of *the* tail section. After these are twisted off, use ~~you~~ *your* fingers to push the lobster meat out of the tail in one piece. Next, remove the black vein~x~ ~~From~~ *from* the tail meat. Finally, before you sit down to enjoy your meal, break open the claws with a nutcracker and remove the meat.

CHAPTER 9, page 80—You Be the Editor

My dog, Bette, is missing. She is a small black poodle with browns eyes. ~~her~~ Her hair is short and curly. Bette weighs 8 pounds and is about one and a half feet ~~foots~~ long. She has a short tail, long, floppy ears, and small feet. She is wear_ing_ a silver collar with an ID tag on it. She is very friendly around people and love_s_ children. I have had Bette for 6 years, since she was a puppy, and I miss her very much. I am offering a $50 reward for anyone ~~which~~ who finds Bette. Please call me at 305-892-7671.

CHAPTER 10, page 92—You Be the Editor

Dear Editor:

In my opinion, it is important for women with small childrens to work outside of the home. First of all, it is ~~to~~ too difficult to be with little kids all day. Womens need_s_ a break from ~~there~~ their kids. Also, a woman who has a career can offer her children mores. It is the quality of time that mothers spend with their children that ~~are~~ is important.

Sincerely,

Lisa Harris

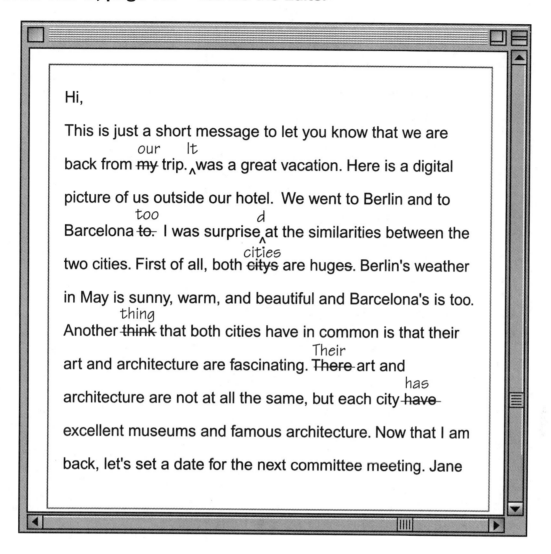

Hi,

This is just a short message to let you know that we are

back from ~~my~~ *our* trip. *It* was a great vacation. Here is a digital

picture of us outside our hotel. We went to Berlin and to

Barcelona ~~to.~~ *too* I was surprise*d* at the similarities between the

two cities. First of all, both ~~citys~~ *cities* are huge~~s~~. Berlin's weather

in May is sunny, warm, and beautiful and Barcelona's is too.

Another ~~think~~ *thing* that both cities have in common is that their

art and architecture are fascinating. ~~There~~ *Their* art and

architecture are not at all the same, but each city ~~have~~ *has*

excellent museums and famous architecture. Now that I am

back, let's set a date for the next committee meeting. Jane

Francisco received a scholarship to study English in the United States. He had a ~~difficulty~~ *difficult* time deciding whether he should attend the English program at Miami Community College in Miami, Florida or Rocky Mountain College in Denver, Colorado. It would be a lot ~~cheapest~~ *cheaper* for him to go to the community college, but he realize*d* that his living expenses would be a lot ~~more high~~ *higher* in the city. Both schools ~~has~~ *have* an excellent reputation, but Rocky Mountain is a much smaller school with a ~~best~~ *better* student/teacher ratio. If he goes to the community college, he will not be as far away from home and he could go home more often~~er~~. He also thought about how he would spend his free time. He might be happier, ~~comfortabler~~ *more comfortable*, and more relaxed in the mountains. Finally, *he* decided to attend Miami Community because the temperature is warmer in Florida and he is used to warm weather and water sports.

DEADLY SURPRISE TORNADO

August 3. The tornado that hit ~~kansas~~ *Kansas* today surprised even the weather forecasters. The violent winds ~~blowed~~ *blew* over 200 miles per hour. ~~Much~~ *Many* crops were destroyed by the storm. Hundreds of people lost ~~his~~ *their* homes or offices because of the high winds and heavy rains. The Red Cross estimates that the killer storm caused many injuries. Also, million*s* of dollars worth of farm animals were killed due to the tornado. *It* will take the people of Kansas ~~many~~ *much* time to recover from the effects of this tornado.

June 10, 2002

Dear Isabelle~~x~~,
^

    I just visited the Morgan Motor Company factory in Malvern, ~~england~~ England and I felt like I was back in the 1920s. There are computers and other modern equipment, but I soon realized that most things have not changed. Morgans ~~is~~ are still made the old-fashioned way. Each one~~s~~ is ~~build~~ built by hand, so no two are exactly alike, and only about ten cars are made per week. That's why there is over a five-year waiting list for a new one. Morgans don't have power steering, ~~a~~ power brakes, or a radio. But, they do have a loyal~~s~~ fan club. Morgan lovers can talk for hours about the thrill of feeling every bump in the road, of listening to the roar of the wind, and of smelling the sweet perfume of burning oil as you drive along. I put my name ~~at~~ on the waiting list for a new Morgan!

Love,

Jackson

1123 Gardner Street

Swansea, Massachusetts 02777

March 2, 2002

Youth Fair Cosmetics Company

234 Philip Place

New York, New York 10028

Dear Sir or Madam~~,~~:

        Youth Fair
I have been using ~~youth fair~~ products for many years and I have always

been very pleased with them. However, last week I bought a bottle of your

        terrible
newest perfume, Rose Petal, and had ~~terribly~~ results. First, it stained my

    d
blouse. It also cause^ my skin to itch and burn. Worst of all, I couldn't stop

    I
sneezing after^ used it. I feel that this product does not meet your standards of

high quality and I would appreciate receiving a refund. I look forward to

hearing from you on this matter in the near future.

Sincerely,
~~sincerely~~^

Charlotte Sherden

Charlotte Sherden

Experts say that the use of electronic mail (also known as "e-mail") is growing

dramatically. According to the Yankee Group, a Boston market-research company,

     e-mail   *the*   *rose*
the number of ~~E-mail~~ users in ^U.S. ~~raised~~ by 60 percent~~s~~ from 5.9 million~~s~~ to 9.4

                       another
million~~s~~ between 1992 and 1993, and it increased ~~other~~ 60 percent in 1993. Billions

                daily
of messages are now transmitted ~~day~~ in North America. That is three times the

                 becoming
number of letters sent by regular mail. E-mail is ~~become~~ more and more valuable

               easier
because it makes communication so much ~~easyier~~.